RETAIL:
THE ART AND SCIENCE

RETAIL:
THE ART AND SCIENCE

The Fundamentals of Retail Buying

Daniel J. Moe

To order additional copies of this book, contact:
Xlibris Corporation
1-888-795-4274
www.Xlibris.com
Orders@Xlibris.com
25964

CONTENTS

Dedicated to Kathi.
Your support and encouragement made this work possible.

FOREWORD

I remember when the executive vice president of Best Buy Retail asked me to teach him about merchandising so that he could better understand the end-to-end picture of a retail marketing organization. An odd request? Hardly. Dozens of people ask me the same question every year. They are the accountants, store managers, advertising associates, and senior leaders. And each of them has recognized that the merchant or buyer is central to any retail organization, and they want some insight into how it works.

The role of the retail merchant/buyer has changed over time, much like the face of retail itself. Think back to the '50s. Department stores (Sears, Wards) and variety (S.S. Kressge, G.C. Murphy, Ben Franklin) dominated the landscape. In the early '60s, the deep discount retailers emerged (Wal-Mart, Kmart, Target). In the '70s, warehouse clubs (Price, Sam's, Costco) came into vogue, and the '80s gave us specialty superstores (Office Depot, Staples, Sports Authority, Best Buy). Megastores followed (Wal-Mart Supercenters, Super Target) in the '90s.

As these formats evolved, so did the role of the merchant. The "old school" buyer selected vendors and items, placed orders, approved payments, negotiated freight terms . . . basically, they did it all. Over time, inventory specialization relieved the merchant of that chore. The role became more focused. Category management became popular in the late '80s and throughout the '90s, especially in the food and drug channels. Today, "integration" is the buzz word. Teaming is fashionable as decision-making authority becomes shared. As these progressions have taken place, retailers have benefited from the development of more generalist leaders, yet I've observed that the core merchant skills and knowledge have greatly diminished. In this observation lies the purpose of this work.

My goal is to have the book work on three levels. First, this work is focused on the basics of merchandising. Each section deals with one of the fundamentals that every merchant needs to understand. I have attempted to be agnostic with each subject. That is, these principles should be applicable to all channels of retail, whether mass, drugstore, specialty store, club, mail order, or grocery.

Next, this effort is meant to be a "how to" book with tangible facts and methods taken from real-world experience within a merchandising environment. I have always found "how to" books to be big on nebulous generalities, filled with grand ideas that are more motivational than they are practical, often leaving the real subject unaddressed. Within these pages, however, the readers will find that "how to" means exactly that. This work offers practical explanations and real lessons that can be applied in retail.

A final objective is to provide a bridge between the manufacturer and the retailer (seller and the buyer). Category management has opened a lot of minds to the idea that collaboration, partnership, and the sharing of ideas can help all parties to better serve the consumer. Still, many sales professionals will readily admit that they do not understand the buyer's mentality. This book should close that gap and enable both buyer and seller to realize that their worlds are actually quite similar.

As for credentials, I do not profess to be an expert on all subjects, but I have drawn on my twenty-plus years of merchandising experience to pull this material together. During that time, I have been a category manager or merchandise manager for numerous product categories, including office furniture, office products, pet supplies, beverages, alcoholic beverages, snack foods, groceries, general merchandise, movies, greeting cards, seasonal, housewares, photography, audio products, wireless technology, and more. I have managed inventory and delivered numerous merchant-related system developments. My most recent experience has been as a vice president of merchandising for Best Buy, where I have managed the audio department, served as the vice president (VP) of merchandising for BestBuy.com, and led a transformation program to instill standardized process across the entire merchant organization.

In addition to my personal experiences, I have interviewed numerous subject-matter experts to help fill in the gaps and make each topic as comprehensive as is appropriate for this work. The material is directed at the new merchant, the seasoned veteran (*everyone can use a dose of the fundamentals*), and those who simply wish to gain a basic understanding of the role of a buyer.

Chapter One

PAYMENT TERMS

Payment terms define the manner and time in which goods are paid for by a customer. When an individual signs up for a credit card, takes on an auto loan, or enters into a home mortgage, the terms of payment are always agreed upon up front (payment due the first of each month, a penalty of 1% if not paid by a certain time, etc.). The terms under which a business pays for its goods are not fundamentally different.

Identifying the terms of payment will often be the first question a buyer asks of a vendor and is often the least revisited of topics. Terms are usually negotiable and are a key element of actual cost. Terms must always be determined and agreed upon before an order is placed. Additionally, the negotiating of favorable terms will often be subject to volume or the "clout" of either party.

For instance, a start-up or small dealer might be required to pay in advance or "at delivery" (COD). Often, however, even small customers can gain basic terms, such as net 30, depending on their financial status. Larger, more established retailers may set minimum terms which they require as a condition of doing business. In the end, terms can be favorable to either the buyer or the seller, and both want that advantage.

The following is an explanation of the most common terms followed by charts on equivalency. These are intended to show the financial impact of payment terms.

Definitions

ADI   After date of invoice. Goods are paid for X number of days after they *ship* from the manufacturer.

ROG   Receipt of goods. Goods are paid for X number of days after they are received by the customer.

EOM   End of month. Invoice payment due by the 10th day of the following month.

EOM +   Invoice payment due by the 10th day of the following month plus extra days.

PROX   Invoice payment due by 10th day of the following month.

PROX +   Invoice payment due by 10th day of the following month plus extra days.

Note: EOM and PROX are the same principle. Various industries use different verbiage.

Examples of Terms

Net 30ADI   Vendor invoice received; invoice payment due within 30 days of date of invoice. The date of invoice is normally the day merchandise ships from the vendor.
Example: Invoice date September 25—payment due October 25.

Net 30 ROG   Vendor goods received; invoice payment due within 30 days.
Example: Merchandise received September 30—payment due October 30.

2% 10 days
Net 30 ADI   A 2% discount if invoice payment is made within 10 days of date of vendor invoice. After 10 days and up to 30 days from shipment of merchandise, invoice payment will receive no purchase discount.

2% 10 days
Net 30 ROG   A 2% discount if invoice payment is made within 10 days of receipt of merchandise. After 10 days from receipt of merchandise and up to 30 days from receipt of merchandise, invoice payment will receive no purchase discount.

2% 30, 1% 60 *Net 70 ADI*	A 2% discount if invoice payment is made within 30 days of receipt of vendor invoice, 1% discount if payment is made within 60 days of receipt of vendor invoice, no purchase discount if paid after 60 and up to 70 days of date of vendor invoice.
2% 30, 1% 60 *Net 70 ROG*	A 2% discount if invoice payment is made within 30 days of receipt of merchandise, 1% discount if payment is made within 60 days of receipt of merchandise, no purchase discount if paid after 60 and up to 70 days of receipt of merchandise.
2% 10 *PROX+30*	Receive vendor invoice (or vendor merchandise) during one month, payment due by the 10th of the following month in order to receive 2% discount.
	Receive vendor invoice (or vendor merchandise) during one month, payment due by the 10th of the following month with additional days to pay in order to receive 2% discount.
2% 10 EOM	Receive vendor invoice (or vendor merchandise) during one month, payment due by the 10th of the following month with additional days to pay in order to receive 2% discount.

Note: EOM/Prox Terms: Most vendors accept a date within the month after which we may think of the receipt as occurring in the next month. Typically this is the twenty-fifth of the month.

Examples of 2% 10 Prox

- Vendor merchandise *received* before the twenty-fifth is to be paid by the tenth of the following month and will receive a 2% purchase discount.
- Vendor merchandise *received* on October 24—Invoice payment to be made by November 10, seventeen days later at 2% purchase discount.
- Vendor merchandise *received* on or after the twenty-fifth of the month will be considered as received in the upcoming

month and is to be paid by the tenth of the following month and will receive a 2% purchase discount. In this case, payment is made by December 10 or forty-seven days after receipt at a 2% discount.

Payment Equivalencies

The following are two views of equivalency. The first illustrates how much money can be made or saved on an order of $50,000. It assumes an 11% interest rate and sets ground zero at net 7 days terms. In other words, assume that you pay the supplier $50,000 within seven days. If you could pay in fifteen days rather than seven, it means an additional $122 of savings. The second equivalency simply defines the many various types of terms in days.

Order Size = $50,000	Interest Rate = 11%
Terms	Incremental Savings Over Net 7
Net 7	0
Net 15	$122
Net 30	$351
1% 10	$546
1% 20	$699
Net 60	$810
2% 10	$1046
Net 90	$1268
2% 60	$1810
3% 30	$1851
2% 90	$2268

Note:

A. Two percent 10 EOM: Placing orders to take full advantage of terms can be an art form. Think of a vendor that sells $100 million/year. If received after the "next month" cut-off date, the purchaser may gain thirty days on $100 million. It could translate into over $918,000 to the bottom line!

B. A $500 million vendor that tries to reduce their terms from
    N 45 to N 30 could cost you $2.3 million! That's fifteen days
    of float on $500 million at 11%.

Equivalent in Days

Rank	Terms	Equivalent in Days
1	2% 30 + 30	120
2	2% 10 EOM + 30	120
3	3% 30	120
4	3% 10 EOM	120
5	Net 60 + 60	120
6	3% 10 Prox	115
7	3% 20	110
8	3% 10/25	110
9	2% 45	105
10	3% 15	100
11	3% 10	100
12	Net 100	100
13	2% 15 EOM	95
14	1% 30 + 30	90
15	1% 30 + 30	90
16	10 EOM + 30	90
17	2% 30	90
18	2% 10 EOM	90
19	Net 90	90
20	Net 10 EOM + 60	90
21	2% 10 Prox	85
22	2% 20	80
23	10/25	80
24	2% 15	75
25	1% 45	75
26	2% 10	70
27	1% 15 EOM	65
28	1% 45	75
26	2% 10	70

27	1% 15 EOM	65
28	1% 30	60
29	1% 10 EOM	60
30	Net 30 + 30	60
31	1% 20	50
32	1% 15	45
33	Net 45	45
34	1% 10	40
35	Net 15 EOM	35
36	Net 30	30
37	Net 10 EOM	30
38	Net 20	20
39	Net 15	15
40	Net 10	10

Many years ago, I worked for the Quill Corporation. Quill was, and still is, the largest mail-order office products dealer in America. Today, the company is owned by Staples, but during my time, the Miller brothers (Jack, Harvey, and Arnold) owned the company.

One of my first jobs at Quill was that of a rebuyer. To those unfamiliar with the term, a "rebuyer" is an inventory position. While a buyer determines the assortment and promotional activity, a rebuyer merely replenishes the merchandise and places the purchase orders. One day, Harry Miller showed up at my desk with a fistful of purchase orders and asked if anyone had ever explained payment terms to me. We both know the answer.

In Harvey's hand were eight orders that I had placed with Bankers Box (this company later changed its name to Fellowes Manufacturing). Truckload orders were placed for Bankers Box every week. Their payment terms were 2% 10 EOM. Harvey explained that 2% 10 EOM meant that we could take a 2% discount on the order if we paid the invoice within ten days of the end of the month (an order received on May 10, paid June 10 received a 2% discount). He further explained that all companies with these types of terms allow for a "cut off" date for companies to process end-of-month terms. In the case of Bankers Box, that date was the twenty-fifth of each month. In other words, orders actually received on the twenty-fifth of the month or later would be considered as having been received on the first of the following month (an order received on May 25, paid by July 10 would receive a 2% discount). It's literally thirty days of float.

So in Harvey's hand were eight purchase orders that had been dated for arrival (by me) for the twenty-second, twenty-third, or twenty-fourth of a month (thus, paid for in about eighteen days). Had I pushed that date to the twenty-fifth, it would have meant an extra thirty days to our terms. Some quick math pointed out that the error was costing the company thousands of dollars each year. Harvey provided a great learning experience that day. I paid close attention to the terms of each vendor from that day forward.

Owned Inventory

Owned inventory has become a popular financial metric for retailers. Payment terms, in combination with inventory turn, will determine owned inventory, and a good merchant should be cognizant of their performance here. When the concept first took hold at Best Buy, people grasped it as a measurement, but most of the merchants felt that they could do little to make an impact on it. In order to make it real for them, I asked the accessories team to focus on owned inventory, and we laid out a plan to improve it.

Our objective: To raise the level of consciousness and create an approach for teams to have impact on this metric.

Step 1   Determine a starting point. We established the current state of our turn, days' equivalencies of payment terms and the owned inventory of products.

Step 2   Set goals. We determined that 51% of our inventory was owned by the company. That is, we have it and it's been paid for. We set a goal to have zero owned inventory within three years. That meant a 33% reduction each year.

      A.   Our year one goal was to reduce owned inventory to 37%.

B.   Targets were set for turnover and terms improvements.

Step 3   Tactics were developed. Some were focused on turn (reduce SKUs, improve case packs) and others on payment terms (identify all current terms, target specific vendors for improvement).

Step 4   Improvements were negotiated.

Step 5   Measure results.

A.   Terms before and after

B.   Recalculate days of turns

Recalculate days of owned inventory

Beginning State

	Turn	Terms in Days	Days Owned Inventory
Video Accessories	4.63	41.46	47.28
Audio Accessories	3.55	49.57	51.66

Goal: Achieve 37%
Owned Inventory

	Turn	Terms in Days	Days Owned Inventory
Video Accessories	4.75	47.0	37.99
Audio Accessories	4.25	53.0	37.43

Actual After 6 months

	Turn	Terms in Days	Days Owned Inventory
Video Accessories	5.10	46.46	34.90
Audio Accessories	4.48	56.57	30.38

The lesson here is that a company's profitability is the culmination of a whole host of factors. Too often, a buyer will focus solely on the cost, retail, and gross margin of the merchandise. Making money work for you can be a key lever in profitability, and the buyer can be integral here.

Let's assume the company has $50 million tied up in accessories inventory when the project began, and that represented fifty days of owned inventory. Reducing the owned inventory to thirty-two days effectively left $18 million in the bank rather than in the warehouse or in the vendor's bank account. At 10%, that's $1.8 million to the bottom line without improving cost or raising a retail price.

Floor Planning

In the constant quest for maximum profitability, the suppliers will always desire to be paid as quickly as possible once their goods have shipped (or before they ship). Conversely, the purchaser will always look to stretch the time in which they actually have the merchandise but have not yet paid for it. Floor planning can be a middle ground. The concept is simple. A third-party financial institution is put in the middle of the vendor/dealer relationship. The purchaser notifies the financial party upon the receipt of goods. They immediately pay the supplier.

- The vendor receives immediate payment and mitigates risk of nonpayment or bankruptcy.
- The retailer or purchaser still receives the benefit of terms. Their cash is not paid out until the specified time of their terms. At this time, it is paid to the floor-plan company.
- A fee is usually paid by the supplier for this service. That's how the financial institution makes money.

    So essentially, it's like a mini-loan. The seasoned merchant, of course, knows that there's no free lunch. Somehow, every cost associated with the vendor finds its way into the cost of goods eventually.

Consignment

Consigned inventories represent an alternative method of vendor financing of inventories. In certain circumstances, it may be advantageous for a buyer to negotiate consignment of vendor inventories rather than standard or even extended payment terms. The use of consignment simply delays the responsibility for payment from the time of receipt to the time of customer sale.

Typically, a knowledgeable buyer will use consignment as part of his or her overall strategy, if appropriate. An example where this proved to be a win-win at Best Buy was on karaoke machines. The category underperformed and never reached its full potential because of open-to-buy constraints within the retailer. The vast majority of sales on this product come in December when every key category is looking for more inventory dollars. In 2000, the vendor agreed to move to consignment. The quantity purchased became a nonissue. The result: more goods were put in the stores, and sales soared almost 200%.

Consignment sounds attractive, but it's not for everybody. System requirements can be taxing, as payment is made according to sales. Also, on fast-turning merchandise with good terms, going to consignment can be a disadvantage. Items like Coke and Pampers can turn twenty-five-plus times for a retailer. With net 30 terms, the retailer has the goods sold and the money in the bank long before payment is due. Forget about consignment here. You're making more money on the turn. A rule of thumb: If you turn inventory eight or nine times or more, you're probably better off taking terms rather than consignment.

Stretch or Float

The term literally means "stretching" payment terms or "floating" your money a bit longer. Some vendors may unofficially extend payment dates. An office-products superstore chain I once worked for kept a list of vendors that we could "float." As buyers talked with sales people, they might discover that while the official terms might be net 30, the vendor's internal policy was to not put a customer on credit hold until payment exceeded sixty days. Here, the buyer might add fifteen days to the terms and pay in forty-five days. Thus, they gain fifteen days of float, and there's no disruption to the flow of orders or goods.

Many large retailers find ways to take the fullest advantage of terms. PharMor, for example, would mail all checks from an obscure post office in Utah; they would claim that payment was postmarked according to the date of terms yet gained three to seven days of float courtesy of the U.S. Postal Service.

As a final note on payment terms, a merchant should always push for the most advantageous terms unless a strategy or circumstance dictates otherwise (i.e., consignment). Additionally, the terms should be reviewed regularly. Do this with line reviews or on an annual cycle. Market conditions change, volume levels change, the vendor's importance in your assortment may change all possibilities for improving your position and bettering the bottom line.

Chapter Two

PORTFOLIO MANAGEMENT

The development of strategy at a category level is a critical activity within any retail organization. Typically, the merchant is charged with developing these strategies and the tactics that drive them. The portfolio process is a structured, fact-based approach that can enable the development of category level strategy. When truly embraced by the organization, portfolio drives the allocation of precious resources such as labor, inventory, ad space, floor space, and more. Additionally, it becomes an effective communication tool as it provides a common language and a framework for the retail organization.

The portfolio process begins with the collection and interpretation of the key data. These data provide a fact-based direction for the role of each category of merchandise. Merchant insights are applied and a "role" for each merchandise grouping is defined. The process is repeated for "intent" (to be explained). Once role and intent are determined, the merchants can develop out their strategy and put their plan into operation. That "operation" will create more data (sales, gross margin, return on space, return on inventory, etc.) for use on the next iteration of the process. Confused? Hang in there. This will all be perfectly clear by the end of the chapter. Let's pull it apart.

Role

The role of a category defines *how* a class of product will create value for the company. Role puts structure around the strategic position of each product grouping. Companies that practice portfolio management typically define four to six "roles" into which categories can be slotted. Best Buy, the nation's leading electronics retailer, has identified five roles for their process.

1. *Primary Business Driver*—It's what Best Buy is know for. PBD categories define the company. They are "top of mind" as the destination for consumer purchases. If taken away, it just wouldn't be the same store. Just for fun, if you think about tools, what retailers come to mind (Home Depot, Lowe's, Sears, and, possibly, True Value)? Tools would be a primary business driver for these retailers. If you think about televisions, which retailers are top of mind (Best Buy, Sears)? Again, these retailers would consider televisions as a primary business driver. Other PBD categories within a Best Buy might be computers, major appliances, digital cameras, and mobile electronics. Key measures of success for PBD categories usually focus on revenue or market share metrics.

2. *Traffic*—These categories have mass appeal to consumers. Typically they are highly visible and price sensitive. They create value by bringing footsteps to the store. Key traffic categories within Best Buy might be music, DVD movies, flash memories, and air conditioners (seasonally). In grocery stores, commodities like milk, eggs, and sodas are traffic drivers. Key measures for traffic categories usually focus on transactions or units sold, inventory turn, and price elasticity.

3. *Profit Generator*—These categories drive profit and support the brand image. Sales are often driven by traffic that is already in the store. Typically these products are less price sensitive, serve a need or solution, and build out a basket. In Best Buy, profit generators might include video accessories, speakers, warranties, joysticks, CD wallets, and so forth. The key measure for success in this role is gross margin.

4. *Convenience*—Unplanned, impulse purchases driven by traffic that's already in the store fall into this grouping. In a Best Buy, products like Coke, magazines, snacks, or films are considered convenience categories. Let's face it, no one goes to a Best Buy to

purchase a Coke or pick up this month's issue of *Sports Illustrated*. They only buy these things because they are in the store and see them. It's an impulse purchase. A key measure for convenience categories would be unit sales or profit.

5. *Emerging*—The nature of electronics is that new gadgets and new technology are constantly coming into the store. At any given time, you can assume that 50 percent of what you see in a Best Buy didn't even exist five to ten years ago. Think about it. In the year 2000, there was no HD television, no satellite radio, no Blu-ray, no photo printers, no HD camcorders, and the list goes on. In order to apply resources to new technologies, Best Buy created this role designation. Emerging categories aspire to be another role. As an example, MP3 players, once an "emerging" business, later became traffic, then PBD, and will someday soon be a profit generator.

Creating the Roles—The creation of a role assignment begins with data collection. These data may include sales history, gross margin trends, market share, and external inputs from reliable industry leaders, marketers like IRI, Neilson, FMI (Food Marketing Institute), NPD, Forrester, and others. Additionally, the vendor community can be a great source of information.

These data are then analyzed in order to suggest an appropriate "role" for specific product categories. For instance, the portable audio category has shown declining sales for several years. As MP3 has grown in popularity, the shift to MP3 devices has significantly impaired the sale of CD players and boom boxes. Industry information and supplier forecasts further support the decline. This may suggest that portable audio devices be classified as profit generator.

As a way to apply more discipline to the process, companies may develop hurdle rates to aid the analysis. That is, a category must sell ten thousand units per month in order to be a traffic category. Or a product category must generate $10,000 gross margin per month in order to be considered a profit generator. These artificial rates have the added benefit of balancing the portfolio. It's natural for all buyers to want their categories to be primary business drivers or traffic. These are sexier roles, and they get more resources. The company, however, needs balance to be viable. Again, the role determines *how* the category produces value.

- Primary Business Driver—*drives brand image*
- Traffic—*brings footsteps*
- Profit Generator—*makes money*
- Convenience—*adds on sales*
- Emerging—*builds the future*

Once an initial pass at role designations is derived from the data and analysis, the important step of applying merchant insights must take place. Thus far, the process has looked into the rearview mirror of information to enable the suggestion of role. The merchant insight is a look forward. It's a critical step. Here's why.

The gaming category is flat. Year over year sales are down. Gross margin rates are steady. Basically, let's pretend that the data suggests it's a profit generator. The merchant, however, knows that Sony will introduce a new PlayStation and Microsoft a new Xbox platform next year. The role may change to PBD.

In the grocery trade, we saw a decline in red meat sales in the eighties and nineties. This trend may have continued, and the data might have suggested a specific role. The merchant, however, saw the low-carb craze and a resurgence of red meat sales before the data suggested it.

The creation of role is a blending of art and science: the science of facts and the art of merchant insights. When this final step is locked down, the determination of intent can begin. Before we dissect the particulars of "intent," a few more thoughts on "role."

In the real world—The process is applicable to just about all retail environments. Think about roles in a bookstore.

- What's a PBD? (hardcover best sellers, paperbacks)
- What's a PG? (bargain books, coffee table books, DVDs)

- What's Traffic? (new releases, Starbucks coffee)
- What's Convenience? (book markers, greeting cards, stationery)
- What's Emerging? (kid's corner, local author section)

Names change, the concept remains—Different industries and different retailers may have role designations that are more appropriate to the business. Still, the concept holds true. This is an approach, a way to allocate resources within the retail environment. Examples of other roles used in grocery or in drug are the following:

- Rehab—*low margin, low sales*
- Under fire—*low margin, intense competition*
- Flagship—*like a primary business driver*
- Cash Machine—*like profit generator*
- Destination—*like flagship or primary business driver*

Roles are different by environment—The role of a category in Best Buy can be completely different in another retailer. DVD movies are a great example. In Best Buy, the category is traffic; in Walgreens, convenience; in Suncoast, a primary business driver; in Target, a profit generator.

Retailer	Film	Batteries	Movies	Television
Best Buy	C	C	T	PBD
Wal-Mart	PG/PBD	T	PG	PBD/PG
Rite Aid	PBD	T	C	C
Radio Shack	C	PBD	N/A	PG/C

Roles change—The portfolio process is repeated annually or semiannually because roles will change as a product moves through its life cycle. Long ago, the Sony walkman was emerging. Once people understood the product, it migrated to traffic. Later it became a profit generator, and today it's probably considered a convenience item.

Product roles can change seasonally as well. A boom box is considered a profit generator all year long; then for two weeks at

Christmas, it becomes a traffic item. Cold medication in the drug channel may be a profit generator in the summer and a traffic driver in the winter months.

Intent

If the role of a category describes how a class of product will create value for the company, the intent will describe *to what degree* that value is to be created. Intent can really only be understood within the context of role. Role + intent will lead to category level strategy development and ultimately to resource allocation. To explain, let's once again look at Best Buy with the intent designations used for the process.

- *Aggressive growth*—The mission is to develop sales, gain market share, and devote the resources necessary to really grow the associated category.
- *Grow*—Utilize appropriate resources to grow the business. This is more moderate than "aggressive grow" and can be interpreted as "continue to grow."
- *Maintain*—Hold your position. The category is important and an integrated part of the mix, but data suggests that further growth will not occur.
- *Harvest*—Reduce the use of resources so that they can be redeployed to the growth areas. Maximize profitability on all levels.
- *Exit*—Developing strategy to be out of the category.
- *Nurture*—Used only in conjunction with emerging categories. Some new businesses have not generated the data necessary to define intent; the retailers must invest resources here.

Now, let's go back. Intent within the context of role will provide direction for category strategy and resource allocation. Think about the DVD movies business within Wal-Mart. Let's assume that they think of this business as a traffic driver / aggressive grow category. What might a retailer do to aggressively grow this business?

Possible answers:

- Give it more space in the store.
- Offer a deeper assortment. Add SKUs.
- Lower prices. Be more aggressive on new releases.
- Add labor in the stores to keep the section orderly and full of stock.
- Acquire space at the checkout lanes for key titles.
- Increase ad space, even lobby for front cover space.
- Arrange for celebrity appearances to key locations.
- Hire more buyers at the corporate office.
- Spend capital to improve department signage.
- Increase the level of inventory.

There is almost an endless list of possibilities if the merchant wants to aggressively grow this business. Now, think of the same category (DVD movies). Change the intent to maintain. What's different?

- Would you increase space for the category?
- Would you increase the investment in inventory?
- Would you lower prices?

When retailers plan their business from the top down, the limits of resources are fairly obvious. There is a defined amount of capital that can be spent. There is only so much space in a store. Inventory must achieve a turn of eight. Payroll must be kept within a specific range. At the heart of the portfolio process, it is understood that resources are finite. In order to invest and grow, select categories a retailer needs to divest and harvest from others. Often these are very hard choices, especially if it means exiting a business.

In the late '90s, Best Buy made the decision to exit the cassette music and minidisc categories. That space in the store was given to DVD movies—a fast-growing category at the time. Categories like grills, fitness equipment, gourmet foods, cookware, air purification, PDAs, typewriters, and so forth have given way to make room for MP3 players, plasma televisions, and networking equipment. If Best

Buy doesn't exit old technology, they would need a store the size of New Jersey to hold everything.

As a child, I remember the marketing tagline for Sears was "Sears has everything." Well, not anymore. When Circuit City exited the appliance business, it was a hard and impactful decision. Applying discipline to portfolio isn't always easy.

When I teach portfolio, I normally pause at this point to reinforce role and intent and make sure the concept is understood. Let us try the following exercise:

Assume you work for one of the following retailers. Identify several categories of merchandise for each role.

- SuperAmerica (other convenience store / gas station)
- Walgreens (other drug chain)
- Golf Galaxy
- Home Depot
- RadioShack
- Bed Bath & Beyond
- Target
- Cub Foods (other grocery chain)

(*Possible answers will appear at the end of this chapter.*)

Primary Business Driver	*Profit Generator*
Traffic	*Convenience*
Emerging	

Going Deeper on Portfolio

Performance Management

Like any process, portfolio can encounter behavioral challenges. Most rewards systems in the retail world focus on sales and gross margin results. In a truly portfolio-driven company, buyers would be rewarded differently based on role and intent. Managers of PBD (primary business driver) categories would be rewarded for sales performance and market share gains. Managers of traffic categories might be rewarded on unit sales. Profit generators would use gross margin dollars. Management needs to realize that the oversight of a PG/Harvest category is as challenging and as important as watching the PBD.

Portfolio Is a State of Mind

Retail product listings are more complex than simple class or category groupings. Therefore, it's important that the merchant understands and applies the principles of portfolio. For example, the category of pet food may be subdivided into dog food (dry), dog food (wet), cat food (dry), cat food (wet), fish, bird, etc. While the retailer may designate "pet food" as a profit generator / maintain, the buyer knows that dry dog food is growing while wet dog food is declining and needs to act accordingly. Car audio is in decline (probably a profit generator / maintain or optimize for Circuit City), but navigation is growing at a fast rate and will need resources.

Generally speaking, role and intent will only be assigned at a category level. The key drivers of this are data. The process is data driven with inputs of market share, category growth forecasts, consumer insights, and more. Few sources provide such information below the category level.

Where to Utilize Portfolio

As the concept permeates a company, the possibilities for applying portfolio are almost unlimited. The most common places to employ portfolio are in the following:

- In stock goals
- Inventory turn goals

- Ad space allocation
- Merchant labor allocation
- Capital spending
- Signage expectations
- Store labor allocation

One caution to consider is that of responsiveness. If a product category is not responsive to a particular lever or resource, it shouldn't receive it. For example, a primary business driver / aggressive grow category may vie for more ad space or more labor. If the addiction yields no positive result, it should be stopped. I often explain to people that an "aggressive grow" intent is not a "get out of jail free" card for resources.

Real World Application

Portfolio can be most effective when it is considered in the actual process of merchandising or retail. Some examples where I've seen very positive long-term results are in the following:

1. *Ad Space*—Some retailers have fairly sophisticated methods for assigning or doling out print ad space to the categories. By using portfolio as a multiplier (PBD = 1.2, PG = 1.0, T = 1.4, C = 0 . . . as an example) in conjunction with responsiveness (actual results from past ads), a retailer can drive the important, growing areas of their business.

2. *Pricing*—Many retailers now employ complex modeling or optimization tools for pricing. How about optimizing primary business drivers for revenue, traffic drivers for unit sales, and profit generators for gross margin dollars?

3. *Resets*—All retailers reset their shelves based on seasonality, assortment changes, or other factors. Can portfolio help to prioritize? Perhaps a primary business driver receives three resets each year while a convenience class receives only one. This expends store labor according to strategic importance. Store space, assortment planning, and labor are also key resources where portfolio can play a part in the formula or methods that allocate the resource.

Balance

It's important to review the balance of assigned roles and intents. If every class of product was designated as traffic, the business would likely fail for lack of profitable categories. The following chart is a good measure for portfolio.

	Category Count	% of sales	% of Units	% of Gross Margin $
Primary Business Driver	15	50%	10%	26%
Traffic Builder	7	19%	50%	16%
Profit Generator	45	27%	30%	54%
Convenience	15	3%	9%	3%
Emerging	3	1%	1%	1%

Notice that a traffic builder represents more of the unit sales (50 percent) than gross margin (26 percent). This makes sense as the mission of traffic builders is to bring foot traffic to the store. Notice also that profit generators are bringing gross margin dollars on a lesser amount of revenue. The same view can be done for intents. A look at the distribution in this manner may prompt challenges or rethinking to be sure that overall business objectives are met.

Versus Category Management

Category Management is a similar approach to managing the retail business at a class or category level. This process was pioneered beginning in 1978 when Procter & Gamble partnered with Schnucks, a St. Louis grocer, to improve their business. This process is very popular and widely used in the grocery and drug channels. The basic process steps are as follows:

- Define the categories
- Set category roles and goals
- Category assessment
- Creation of a scorecard
- Determine category strategy

- Develop tactics
- Implementation
- Monitor and review results

Since volumes have been written on category management, I will skip that part and simply point out the key differences between category management and portfolio.

1. Both processes are pervasive and need alignment from the top of the company.
2. Portfolio is focused on resource allocation while category management is focused on achieving defined category goals (performance against a scorecard).
3. Portfolio is very much an internal process. Category management is a collaboration with the vendors (typically a category captain is assigned).
4. Both used internal (sales, gross margin, average, selling price) and external (market share, share of wallet, consumer insights) data to develop strategy.
5. Portfolio is often most effective when class definition and standards don't exist. Category management is most effective where these do exist. The grocery and drug trades have a strong industry group (FMI, the Food Marketing Institute) that clearly defines product classes for the trade. As a result, dry dog food is dry dog food for everyone. While it sounds simple, other retail segments like hardware, electronics, toys, and others are less structured. Is an MP3 player a portable audio product or a computer product? It depends.

Lastly, category management is very focused on consumer insights and consumer data. Again, food and drug have been far ahead of other industries in the collection of consumer data. Companies like ACNielsen and IRI have been gathering purchasing information for decades while such work is only beginning in other channels.

A Final Word

The process of portfolio management can be an effective way to manage the retail environment. Once a company has defined its high-level strategy (Nordstrom stands for service; 7-Eleven stands for convenience) or what it stands for, portfolio can bring focus to managing precious resources and defining category level strategy. To understand the process, one must realize that portfolio management is as much a state of mind as it is a process. It is not possible to have rules for all resource allocation within a company. So it's important that merchants apply the principles of portfolio when a clear definition is not available.

Portfolio is foundational. The retail landscape changes rapidly, and many argue that we are quickly moving from a box-selling world to one of personalization, even experiential. Just a few years ago, the Home Depot was a "do-it-yourself" store. Today it's more about "You can do it. We can help." Best Buy is focused on complete solutions, the customer experience. In this new evolution, some think a portfolio process is too product centric and not relevant. I disagree. The road to solution, experience, and service cannot abandon the fundamentals and process disciplines of retail. Portfolio has never been more relevant.

Possible answers to exercise:

ROLES IN VARIOUS RETAIL BUSINESSES

	PBD	Traffic	Profit Generator	Convenience	Emerging
Walgreens	Pharmacy	Coke	Greeting Cards	Movies	Holiday Inventory
	Film Lab	Milk	Cosmetics	Candy	Drive-thru
SuperAmerica	Gas	Lottery	Snacks	Gum	Propane
	Oil	Cigarettes	Pet Food	Magazines	Car Wash
Golf Galaxy	Golf Clubs	Golf Balls	Clothing	Club Covers	Lessons
	Putters	New Driver	Shoes	Video	Demo Centers
Home Depot	Tools	Lawn Fertilizer	Window Treatments	Snow Shovel	Services
	Paint	Light Bulbs	Flooring	How-to Books	Specialists
Cub Foods	Produce	Milk	Pet Food	Flowers	Olive Bar
	Meats	Coke	Prepared Foods	Magazines	Lens Crafters

Chapter Three

PRICING

Pricing is perhaps the most complicated issue within retail. For that reason, most companies develop a very specific policy or philosophy around pricing. In this way, all merchants, executives, store associates, essentially the entire company can clearly understand the company's position on price and align to it. When clearly defined, the issue is simplified. But make no mistake. Pricing practice defines a company.

The subject of price finds its way into almost every topic the merchant will encounter. For our purposes here, I hope to define many of the elements of pricing, explain pricing philosophy through actual examples, tie pricing to strategy, address pricing against competition, and leave the reader with a sound, fundamental appreciation of the purpose, complexity, and importance of pricing. To begin, there are some basic definitions that may enhance one's understanding of the topic. In an attempt to not rival Webster or Thorndike, I've culled a lengthy list down to the essentials.

Definitions

List, MSRP

List Price or Manufacturer's Suggested Retail Price are benchmarks established by the manufacturer. The "list" is thought to be the fair market value of a product.

Establishing such a benchmark can trigger pricing strategies or policy. Retailers may claim "20% off list." That means 20% off the benchmark price established by the manufacturer.

Suppliers often use list price as a benchmark for selling their goods to retailers or dealers. Assume a three-ring binder has a stated list price of $12.95. A manufacturer might offer the basic dealer a "50 off list" discount. In other words, they would bill the dealer $6.475 per binder purchased ($12.95 x .5 or 50% off list).

A larger retailer might purchase the same product at a 50/20 discount or $5.675 per binder ($12.95 x .5 x .8). Volume speaks loudly. A wholesaler, in turn, might purchase the product at a 50/20/20 discount or $4.54 per binder.

EDLP

Everyday Low Price is a simple philosophy employed by many retailers. Products are sold at one low price every day. The promise here is that you don't need to wait for a sale.

The most visible examples of EDLP are Wal-Mart, warehouse clubs (Costco, Sam's, Price) and category superstores (PetsMart, Office Depot, Staples).

A great advantage to an EDLP program is that a company gains efficiency by not repricing and printing and placing new signs every time the retail price goes up or down. A disadvantage can be that they may be beat on price when a competitor lowers their retail for a sale.

Hi/Lo

Hi/Lo is a term associated with retailers that have a regular everyday price that is discounted or put on sale in order to attract customers. Grocery chains, drug store chains, and department stores often embrace this practice.

MAP

Many manufacturers (especially in consumer electronics) have established MAP (Minimum Advertised Price) policies. Initially, these programs were developed to discourage price wars that constantly eroded retail prices. XYZ Electronics would offer a low price. ABC Electronics would advertise an even lower price, maybe even at cost in order to drive traffic or steal market share.

Soon XYZ would retaliate and possibly sell an item below cost, driving products to commodity status.

MAP is a fairly simple concept. The manufacturer will offer special incentives to dealers. These incentives will be withheld if the retailer does not abide by the Minimum Advertised Price policy of the manufacturer. In some categories, like movies, a break in MAP can cost the retailer millions of dollars in supplier support. Note that the manufacturer does not dictate what a product can be sold for. That would be illegal or price fixing; they merely incentivize people to maintain a minimum retail when advertising the product.

AOS or EOS

All on Sale or Everything on Sale is a claim that every item in some grouping (all TVs, all pencil sharpeners, all diapers or all P&G diapers) is on sale. State laws most often require that such a claim be substantiated by at least a 5% reduction from regular price (in Massachusetts, 10% off is the minimum required).

Gross Margin

Gross margin is a way to express the profit in selling an item(s).

Retail price - Cost = the gross margin of an item
Gross margin ÷ Price = GM percent
Example: Price is $6; Cost is $4; thus, GM is 33.3.

Pricing Policy and Philosophy

Have you ever wondered how that roll of film came to be priced at $4.69? The art and science of applying the selling price can be the most challenging and risky part of the buyer's job. Price it too high, it may not sell. Too low, you may go broke. That's why most companies provide guidance on how to set retails within their environment.

It makes good sense, as stores are built according to a business model. Macy's, as an example, offers a delightful experience, is typically in a mall, and they offer a high degree of service. Compare that to a Sam's Club. Stack 'em high and let 'em fly. Nothing fancy, charge a membership fee, no bags at checkout, no credit cards, and no helpful service in the aisles. The prices at Macy's need to account for the services you expect. They work on high margins and are prepared to take steep markdowns as needed to move out seasonal goods. A warehouse club is a formula business. The original theory was to work on a 9% gross margin. This covers cost, and they make money on the membership fees and inventory turn.

Pricing guidance is a way to provide a framework for success within a particular environment. A good policy serves as a tool for the merchant and others. To further illustrate this point, I'll offer two views of a pricing manual or policy.

The first is a hybrid that I employed in a catalog environment in South Florida and has roots in mail order. The company was Jaffe Stationers. The products sold were office products. In this unique industry, almost all the items have a manufacturer's suggested retail price associated with them (list price). Additionally, the industry is prone to offering quantity discounts. For example, buy one case of copy paper for $29.99, five cases for $27.99/case, ten cases for $25.99/case. These quantity breaks are referred to as "columns" for price.

The second example is applicable to a large specialty retail store. In each, please note that specific direction is provided on how to set retails. The policies are actually manuals and very detailed. The reader should focus on the big picture; pricing can make or break the company.

Catalogs/Mail Order Business
Company A Pricing Manual

PURPOSE: To ensure that pricing, pricing policies, and pricing techniques are understood and adhered to by all employees involved in the pricing process. This manual's guidelines are not intended to be followed "off a cliff." The guidelines are intended to be interpreted and adjusted, if need be, to reflect changing market conditions and practices. Pricing must, at all times, convey to the customer an image of integrity, honesty, fairness, and clarity.

1. *Pricing Philosophy*

The overall goal is this: Be perceived by the customer as a company that promotes quality products at very competitive prices. This is not a cheap house but a discount house. All items shown should be discount priced off of manufacturer's list prices. In the case of private label (no list price exists for private-label goods), all items should be discounted off of a comparable item's manufacturer's list price. Prices on private-label products should normally be much greater values than even discount pricing on brand names. While price is important, the company should not be striving to show low prices by carrying cheap products. We should, however, offer good commercial-quality or top-quality products at *significantly* lower prices than usually available through other office products and/or mail-order dealers.

Low prices should be a result of our volume plus better negotiating, better sourcing, and more efficient operation.

Pricing should be very competitive, as the company wants to continue to build its image as a low-cost supplier. The company does not want to hold up a pricing umbrella that allows our competition to grow and prosper. Pricing should be aggressive based on buying and operating advantages. These advantages must allow us to realize good margins as well as pass on part of the buying advantages to the customer to remain very competitive in the marketplace yet very profitable.

Retails should not just match the competitors' pricing but should try to beat them. Avoid being part of the game where everyone is trying to price the same as everyone else, or just a few pennies lower. Quantity, combination, and deal-pricing techniques will help set the company aside from the crowd. Show significant savings where possible and still meet profitability objectives. The company should be willing to *lead* the market down in areas where we can, instead of being part of the group that holds prices up.

We do our own pricing. Manufacturers do not have a say in how we price merchandise, either regular or promotional. Listen to their input or concerns, but in the final analysis, we make our own decisions.

2. *Specific Pricing Policies and Guidelines*
   Starting points for establishing regular pricing should always be

   A. Defining your product cost. Before you begin pricing your products, you must first establish your "laid in" or "sell cost."

      i. Net Invoice Cost—The amount we pay the manufacturer for a product (the pure cost of the item). This can be any of the following:

         a. A net cost based on a quote
         b. A discount off list. (List price of a 1" binder is $10. A 50/20 discount equals a cost of $4.)
         c. A published cost/price list.

      ii. Inbound Freight—As merchandise comes in, the transportation costs are handled in one of three ways:

         a. Prepaid—When a vendor ships prepaid, the company does not see a freight bill. The freight is accounted for in the cost of goods.
         b. Prepay and Add—Under these terms, the company is billed separately for freight. The charge is usually added to the invoice, and the vendor normally controls the carrier. Charges must be broken down to the item level in order to add the cost of freight to the product.
         c. Collect—When a vendor ships collect, the freight charges are separate and in addition to the cost of goods. However, we control carrier selection and routing.

      iii. Additional Cost Factors
         These "factors" may add to or detract from the true net cost of an item. Examples may include the following:

a. Tooling Charges—When purchasing a proprietary item, a short-term charge to pay for tooling may be factored into the cost of goods.

b. Private label or packaging charges

c. Shrink Wrapping—As an example, the company may purchase business forms in bulk quantities and repackage them in lesser quantities for resale.

d. Handling Charges

e. Duty, Insurance, or Ocean Freight—seen on imported goods

iv. Laid In or Sell Cost—The sum of the net invoice cost plus inbound freight plus or minus any extras that may alter it. Sell cost is the *final* cost at the point we will sell the item. Gross profit is calculated from sell cost.

3. *Determining Your Selling Price.*

A. Points A-E can help you determine what your selling price should be.

B. Discount off manufacturer's list price. A list price indicates a product's relative retail selling value suggested by the manufacturer. When pricing off manufacturer's list, always shoot for being 15 to 20% or more off the manufacturer's list price. There are exceptions to this 15 to 20% off manufacturer's list rule. One would be on products where there is a very short discount to the company. The other exception would be on products that carry a very high manufacturer's list. In this case, discounts may be as high as 40% off manufacturer's list in first-column pricing.

C. What is competition charging for the same or similar product? If competition is mail order, check to make sure who is paying the freight (the dealer or the customer) to the customer and consider that in pricing.

D. What are similar products priced at in the assortment? In other words, pricing on a "better grade" will be greatly influenced by what pricing exists on the "economy grade" and "best," top-of-the-line-grade product within the product mix. As an example, if economy copy paper is priced at $19.99/case and standard copy paper sells for $24.99/case, the addition of a premium grade might be priced at $29.99/case. Pricing it too close to "standard" copy paper would not offer enough differentiation for the consumer.

E. Unit of measure, inner packs and outer packs, must have a strong bearing on how you establish your pricing columns. The cost of handling an item in the warehouse is to be considered at all times. See the example below.

	Mfg Suggested List Price	Company Discount Pricing		
		1 EA	12 EA	48 EA	144 EA
Acco 1" Binder-BK	$5.00	3.99	3.74	3.49	2.99
Acco 1" Binder-BE	$5.00	3.99	3.74	3.49	2.99
Acco 1" Binder-RD	$5.00	3.99	3.74	3.49	2.99
Acco 2" Binder-BK	$7.50	5.99	5.59	5.24	4.99
Acco 2" Binder-BE	$7.50	5.99	5.59	5.24	4.99
Acco 2" Binder-RD	$7.50	5.99	5.59	5.24	4.99

Notes:

1. The first column is a 20% savings off the list price.
2. The buyer can claim "Save up to 40%" or "Save 25-40%."
3. Each column offers a deeper value to the consumer.
4. Retails are price pointed. That is, 20% off of $5 is actually $4. The price is set at 3.99 to break that $4 barrier and appear more compelling.
5. If binders were purchased in a "discount from list" fashion, cost for the 1" binder might be $1.80 (a 50/20/10 discount or $5 x .5 x .8 x .9 = $1.80). At $3.99, the gross margin is 54.88. It drops as low as 39.7 in the fourth column.

6. Columns are all divisible by twelve. Binders are packaged twelve per case.

4. *Other "basic rules" to consider that will have an effect on your pricing decisions.*

   A. A minimum order for a product should be the same as the unit of measure. Exceptions should be discussed and approved. For example, if the unit of measure on pens is "dozen" and the product is packed in dozens, then the first pricing column would be one dozen and not one each.

   B. A basic strategy is to have four pricing columns. Those products having more or less should be discussed and approved up front. Machines (phones, computers), for example, are generally priced using one pricing column. Furniture is generally priced using one and sometimes two pricing columns. Make sure that when establishing your pricing columns, you make them compatible with the products' inner and outer packs.

   C. The gross profit margin difference between each column of four-column pricing should be at least two percentage points. In the binder example, it's five.

   D. *Sale* pricing on four-column pricing should normally be just below the fourth-column regular price. If the fourth-column regular price is $19.97, then your sale price should usually be just below (i.e., 19.96 or 19.88). The sale price of $19.96 or $19.88 would be for goods bought in the first pricing column. Binders, as an example, might be put on sale for $2.88 each.

   E. Avoid zeros and fives as price endings. An exception to this rule would be on products in which you show display price in each, but the base unit of measure is a larger quantity, such as a box or roll. Blank Media, for example, are priced in boxes of ten, but the display price is shown in each (0.59 each or 5.90 per box of ten).

F. Price point where possible. Try to make sure you break a dollar amount when applicable. For example, 1.98 instead of 2.03. Be careful on how much margin you lose doing this. On low-priced items, the profit margin lost by moving just pennies can be significant.

G. When promoting manufacturer-brand products (not private label), the reduction in selling price uses a "save story" showing a percentage of dollar amount off the suggested manufacturer's list price. For example, "Save 25% off manufactures list price."

H. When promoting private-branded products, the reduction in selling price is a "cut story" showing an extra percentage or dollar amount off our every day low price. "Cut 25% off our regular price."

I. When showing various savings in a price chart, it is not permissible to use the greatest savings story in this manner, "Save *up to* 55% off manufacturer's list." If you have six items in a chart, five of them are 40% off list and one is 55% off list, you should advertise it as 40% off list. If your most popular item is 55% off list, you can advertise 40 to 55% off list. It is important to be honest. If you want to go with one cut or save story rather than a range, it is permissible to understate your story. Let's not mislead the customer.

J. Cut or save stories should be at least a 15% reduction, as a general rule. Again, there are exceptions to this rule where margins are too low or where a whole house event is running. Note: A "whole house event" might be a financing sale or "All Furniture on Sale" or the like stories. Remember, if it is a cut story, indicate "cut an *extra* amount off our already low prices."

K. When doing a save story with huge "savings," such as save 50, 60, or 70% off list, you tend to lose credibility. In the event where you have a large savings, try to prove it to the customer.

L. You do not necessarily have to say cut or save at all. You may just show the sale price.

M. When putting together component products to make "deals" (i.e., a combination of items on sale for a single-display price), make sure the deal is a bona fide savings to the customer. Customers should not be able to duplicate or improve upon deal pricing by buying the items separately (particularly when one or more of the components are on sale separately).

N.   Finally, pricing is not a science, it is an art. In most cases, common sense should prevail. In all cases, strive for honesty and clarity.

Having had a policy that clearly defines the company's pricing methods was a great tool. As new merchants, store managers, and other key people joined the company, they were able to quickly understand our positioning. Here is another example.

Specialty Store Chain
Company B Pricing Manual

I. Purpose/Strategy: As a category superstore, the company has taken the position of being the price leader in the marketplace. A number of factors are known to influence the decision on where to shop. Chief among them are location, breadth of assortment, availability of product, the shopping environment, and price. The company believes that it will deliver on all of these key motivators but believes that establishing the image as a price leader will differentiate us from the competition.

In general, customers are only aware of the price on the most visible commodity-like items. Examples throughout retail might be a two-liter bottle of Coke, gasoline, cigarettes, diapers, Crest toothpaste, a four-pack AA batteries, and so forth. In this environment, the company will establish a list of the most highly identifiable items (power items). By always being the best price on these power items, the company will establish a halo effect and influence the customer's perception that we offer overall value.

The company will offer one low everyday price on merchandise. We do not put items on sale. We do not offer volume or quantity discounts.

On non-power items considered to be less price sensitive, the company should always offer a great value when compared to more traditional, non-superstore competitors. Also, against direct competition, the company should always remain competitive on these items.

II. Retail Guidance for Company B
   A.   Pricing Committee

The company has established a pricing committee (members from merchant, finance, and store operations and inventory departments), which meets monthly to review power items and hear recommendations from the business.

   B.   Power Items

The merchant group will identify the key driving items that consumers will identify and use to gauge the relative driving of overall pricing. Those items will become "Power Items." The list should be the top 100 most identifiable price-sensitive items.

    1.   Does the sales velocity justify an item being on the list?
    2.   Is the item regularly advertised within the industry?
    3.   Is the item consumable? That is, can we expect multiple or repeat purchases of the item?
    4.   Is the price high? Often, higher-priced goods are shopped around, as the opportunity to save is greater.

These items will be shopped quarterly against all competition. They will be priced to win in the marketplace, even if winning means a low or negative gross margin.

   C.   Price Zones

The company has established pricing zones as follows:

    1.   Base Zone—The base zone is to be established for all items. It is the foundational retail price for the chain.

2. Mass Market Zone—The mass market is defined as Wal-Mart, Kmart, Target, and any super regional chains that compete in our space. Retail information placed here will override the base-zone pricing. Mass-market-zone pricing should be used when a store is within two miles of a mass competitor that is considered to be the primary competition.

3. Warehouse Club Zone—Sam's Club, Price Club, and Costco would fall into this category. On all power items, the company will meet or beat the posted club price. While clubs do charge a membership fee and a markup for nonbusiness customers, the price impression is the sign. We will match it.

4. Other Specialty Chains—Where the primary competition is, another like specialist use this zone. Focus on the power items is critical, but price adjustments may need to go beyond this list when faced with specialty chain competition.

5. No Comp Zone—In these markets where there is no real competition, there is often an opportunity to move prices up. This zone will enable merchants to raise retails and maximize gross margin.

III. Setting Retails

    A. Manufacturers List Prices (MSRP)

        Most manufacturers publish a suggested list price for their items. This MSRP will be a benchmark for printed materials (catalogs, circulars) and for any claims of savings.

    B. Power Items

        The company will price competitively by price zone or by chain base price on all power items. That is, we will meet or beat recognized competition on these goods. We cannot be beat, as these items establish our price image.

    C. Greeting Cards—All greeting cards will be priced and signed as "Save 25-50% Every Day." Use the following chart:

Preprinted Card Price	Our Price	Save
$1.00	.75	25%
$1.25-$2.50	.87-1.75	30%
$2.75-$4.00	1.65-2.40	40%
$4.25 and up	2.12 and up	50%

D. Magazines

All magazines will be sold at 10% off every day. The discount will be taken at the register.

E. Books

Best sellers, as determined by the New York Times bestseller list, will be priced at 35% off the cover price. All other vendor-supplied books will be sold at 15% off every day.

Exceptions may be promo buys such as a dictionary for back to school. Price these either by competition or by the category gross margin.

F. Special Purchase Pricing

The pricing guideline for special purchases is that they must offer excellent value to the customer. This includes being priced to sell out in sixty days or less. Be sure to allow ample gross margin to offset the markdowns that may be necessary to sell off any remaining inventory.

G. Clearance Pricing

Slow-selling merchandise stagnates the inventory, takes up valuable selling space, reduces return on investment, and in most cases, detracts from the value of our image. Clearance merchandise are those items that we want to move out of our assortment. In our vendor negotiations, we will ask all vendors for advance notice of the discontinuance of merchandise. In addition, if merchandise is discontinued, we will ask to return the merchandise back to the vendor at no cost. Or in the case of a vendor replacement, we will aggressively ask for markdown money to help us clear out the merchandise to be replaced.

In the case where merchandise is discontinued and we elect not to return the merchandise to the vendor, our policy is to mark the merchandise down aggressively. Once tagged as "Closeout" or "Clearance," the merchant cannot (by law) raise the price back up.

H. Ad Pricing

All items in an ad are always priced at the every day low retail. Items are never on sale.

IV. Price Pointing

Merchants should always look to create value through appropriate price points. On all items below $100, refrain from cent endings of "0," "5," or "9." These are to "retailish" and do not scream value. Use the following chart as a guide:

0—Do Not Use
1—6.51, 37.81, 82.41
2—3.62, 34.42, 58.82
3—7.23, 42.63, 86.53
4—1.44, 14.74, 73.24
5—Do Not Use
6—5.76, 35.26, 97.56
7—6.27, 41.37, 85.87
8—3.58, 26.18, 79.08
9—Do Not Use

When items retail for $100 or more, we will use whole dollar increments in pricing. No cents.

Again, a well-defined, detailed pricing policy will provide the organization with direction and consistency. If the strategy is every day low price (EDLP), the buyer knows clearly that the price is not cut for an ad. If policy states that all discontinued merchandise is reduced 30%, that's clear direction, and the likelihood of execution is high.

In the early '90s, PharMor, a deep-discount retail drug chain was the darling of retail. This fast-paced, fast-growing organization had a rather unique pricing philosophy. After extensively studying the grocery and drug trades, founder Mickey Monus determined that cost plus 162/3 was the "magic" formula to produce an incredible price impression. This formula was combined with the "deal buying" philosophy (only purchase items offered on deal or promotion from the vendor) to produce tremendous consumer value. Of course, select products were excluded: greeting cards, alcoholic beverages (state mandates usually control prices), pharmacy products, and a core of "meet competition" items like diapers, Crest toothpaste, and others that might be sold at or below cost.

This simple strategy made pricing the items quite simple (cost x 1.166). It did not, however, work. PharMor no longer exists today. Still, the example of clear direction to the organization stands as a good model.

Another more common strategy is a modified EDLP. In this circumstance, a retailer takes an everyday low-price posture but offers sale pricing or other promotional events to create excitement. Toys R Us and Best Buy are examples. Best Buy offers every day low prices, touts a price guarantee, yet occasionally put an entire category "on sale" (all camcorders, all vacuum cleaners) or provide a special incentive (free delivery, free installation, eighteen months' financing) to create excitement.

In the end, a company's price strategy is the essence of the business. It helps to create an identity for the company. Does "Always Low Prices, Always" come to mind?

Price Pointing

Price pointing is the way in which a company presents the retail price to their customers and is often very specific and purposeful. As seen in the superstore example, their policy did not allow for the prices to end in 0, 5, or 9. This is actually a modified warehouse-club methodology.

Warehouse clubs (Sam's, Costco, Price) were originally conceived as a cost plus environment in which all the services and niceties were eliminated in order to deliver one thing—low cost. Most clubs use gigantic racking and stack pallets directly on the floor. It's the most cost-efficient way to handle merchandise. In addition to this, they may employ the following strategies:

- They hang up or post a price sign rather than price each item. It saves money.
- Clubs sell bulk packs or larger quantities. It feeds the perception that buying in quantity must be cheaper.
- They don't take credit cards (although some have broken this rule). Credit costs money.
- They don't carpet or tile the floor. Consumers push oversized carts around on concrete floors, under high ceilings. It serves up a low-cost ambience.
- Also, clubs price point to create the perception that every nickel has been squeezed out of cost to give you the greatest possible value. It's not uncommon to see copy paper at $29.06, or a broom at $6.72, a six-pack salsa at $9.21. They avoid 0s, 9s, 8s, and 5s believing that $9.99 or $7.95 feels too traditional. It's a strategy.

Note: *Caveat emptor* (buyer beware)! Sometimes clubs offer no real value. Check the giant box of three cereals. When compared on a cost-per-ounce basis, the basic grocery store often wins on price. The perception, however, screams value. Also, clubs add 5% at checkout over the posted price for nonbusiness members. Just another catch.

Often, a retailer might use price endings to denote the status of an item. In this way, everyone, including store personnel, can identify it easily. Here are some examples:

- all discontinued merchandise ends in .50
- all regular priced merchandise ends in .99 or .95
- sale merchandise might always end in .88

The best guidance I can offer around price pointing is that barring a stated company position (like warehouse clubs), the merchant should always strive to maximize gross margin and break natural barriers: $99 is more palatable than $101, or $29.88 is more natural than $30.06.

Pricing Against Competition

Pricing against competition is a concern for all major retailers. Perhaps the most common practice employed is the use of price zones. Price zones are logical groupings of stores that share a defined commonality and can, therefore, offer "like pricing" on items. Price zones can be geographic in nature but are more commonly determined based on competition. More sophisticated retailers can actually zone their prices by product category. Walgreens might be an example.

Liquor, beer, and wine are subject to state regulations. These products are only purchased through distributors (never direct from the winery or brewery) by law. To further complicate this business, each state has its own rules and laws governing the sale of alcoholic beverages. In Michigan, the state requires a minimum gross margin of 6%. In Ohio, beer has a minimum mark up of 20%; wine, 33%; and hard liquor can only be purchased in a state liquor store (retailers love Ohio because of this guaranteed profitability). In West Virginia, the retailer also serves as the wholesaler to restaurants and will offer two-tier pricing. In Illinois, anything goes. In this circumstance, price zones are set up geographically in order to accommodate these variations by state.

Zoning by competition is the more prevalent method. In this scenario, each store is viewed in terms of its location and the competition it must deal with. A typical drug-store chain might zone as follows:

01   Base Zone (base pricing according to company strategy)
02   Walgreens (key competition is Walgreens)
03   Rite Aid (key competition is Rite Aid)
04   Mass Merchant (key competition is Wal-Mart, Kmart, or Target)
05   Non-compete (no direct competition; opportunity to raise price)

Another sophisticated approach to addressing competition is the "anything goes" method. Some chains have the capabilities to vary pricing by item, by store. This allows the company to react to competition at a local level.

Electronics retailers often price in this manner. Buyers initially establish retails at the corporate office. The buyer is charged with knowing his/her product category in-depth, including the marketplace retails. After initial setup, a pricing department monitors competition and is authorized to adjust the retail price to the benefit of the consumer. This occurs in two ways, adjusting the price based on ads in the marketplace or by actually shopping the competition.

This practice of adjusting price by store, by item, can appear costly on the surface, but it is believed to be a great branding benefit. If it says "Best Buy" on the sign, you will get a best buy in the store. As a result, consumer trust is built over time. Also, smart consumers will "get it." That is, always shop at the Target store that's near a Wal-Mart. You'll get the selection, ambiance, and service of a Target and the price of a Wal-Mart (they match Wal-Mart's).

Additional Pricing Practices and Nuances

1. Price-related claims. Most retailers establish rules to support any price claims that they may tout. These rules need to cover any legal issues or state requirements. For this reason, most major retailers employ a compliance person or department which will interpret claims and advise the merchant group on what is or isn't legal or appropriate. As an example, "Lowest Advertised Price of the Year" is a bold claim and can generate excitement from the consumer. Of course, the claim must be true, and there are rules around the use of such a claim.

2. Price progression or ladders. When a product line or category has a natural progression in value, the retail prices would normally follow accordingly. Think of good, better, best. One logically assumes "best" would cost more than "better," "better" more than "good"!

Good	Store brand 200 ASA film, 24x	.99/roll
Better	Kodak 200 ASA film, 24x	1.99/roll
Best	Kodak Gold 200 ASA film, 24x	2.49/roll

3. Value Pricing. A common practice in grocery stores. This pricing offers consumers a better value when purchasing in quantity.

> Frozen grape juice   2 for $5 (reg. 2.99 each)
> Buy one get one free
> Buy two get one free
> 25% more

4. Traffic Pricing. Using price to drive customers to a store. The aggressive price needs to be associated with an identifiable item for the particular store. That is, a great price on coffee at Office Depot doesn't really work. A great price on copy paper would be meaningful.

> Coke or Pepsi   .79/2 liter for grocery
> Cigarettes for a convenience store

5. Line Pricing. The practice of pricing a category of products or "a line" in the same manner. For example, every item priced at a specified gross margin based on cost. Or every item is priced at the same discount from list.

> All Greeting Cards 25% Off

This practice is fairly common for SKU intensive product categories. Many drug chains line price greeting cards or set up a standard discount in their registers rather than trying to price ticket or print a shelf label for them. Not only are there a lot of cards in an everyday assortment, but the seasonal changes (Christmas, Easter, Mother's Day, etc.) make other methods prohibitive and inefficient. Many retailers apply similar strategies to books, magazines, music, and movies.

DVD new releases	30% off
DVD catalog	10% off
All best sellers	25% off
Other books	10% off

One prerequisite for this practice is that a benchmark (or a list price) needs to be present. Note: All books have a preprinted cover price, all greeting cards have a preprinted retail price at the back.

6. Internet Pricing. Retailers on the Internet (click 'n' mortar) can face numerous challenges with price. A price posted on the Internet is visible to anyone visiting the site. Consider that most major retailers zone prices or react; it becomes quickly apparent that net prices may not match the retail posted in the store. As companies develop their pricing strategy for online stores, they need to ask several questions:

    a. Should the website match retail prices in store?

    b. Can the web price be lower than the store? If so, will customers ask for the lower web price if shopping in the store?

    c. Will promotions align between the stores and the Internet?

The key here is to understand that the Internet is a different channel, more mail-order-like than a retail store. Promotions such as "Free Delivery" are more powerful on the web than in stores.

One simple solution that many retailers have adopted is to treat the Internet as their base-price zone. Basically, it becomes the high-price zone. If consumers see a lower price in the store, they'll generally be more accepting of it.

Modern Pricing Tools

Many of the concepts in this chapter are a legacy of twentieth-century retailing. The policies, price pointing, and other practices are really ways to provide guidance within a subject that is very much an art form. In the twenty-first century, however, science has come to the forefront in the field of pricing. New modern tools are capable of channeling incredible amounts of data and can apply sophisticated elasticity modeling to create retail prices.

One example is referred to as price optimization. It is the process of combining business goals and business rules with consumer price sensitivity to determine the best possible combination of prices to meet financial and consumer goals. It's a tool to exploit items for improved performance while building and sustaining a positive price image.

As is often the case, the grocery channel was the first to experiment with these options, but other retail segments soon followed. The process is fairly simple.

1. The tool (software) is loaded with SKU level, transaction data, usually a full year or more of data are gathered; with a broad lengthy base the software can identify any price adjustments and capture the result in demand. Think about every transaction on every SKU of a category for every store for a year. It's easy to understand why computers are needed to create these data rather than people.
2. Rules that pertain to the category are defined. A rule might be "All private label products should be 10 percent off list," or "Do not raise any price more than 5 percent."
3. Modeling is run, and the results are reviewed.
4. Prices are implemented and results monitored.

It's important to note that "optimization" is not about raising prices. It's about monitoring the opportunities and achieving business goals. For example, a "good" folding table sells for $49 (100 units/month). A "better" folding table sells for $79 (10 units/month). The "best" folding table sells for $84 (50 units/month). The step from "good" to "better" of $30 is too great. Why spend $30 for the better table when $40 gets you the best? Here, a lower price, say $69, would create a more logical step and sell more tables and deliver additional gross margin.

These types of tools are now being applied to regular price, clearance price, and promotional priced goods and changing the landscape of the pricing function.

Chapter Four

CREATING AN ASSORTMENT

Developing an assortment is the most basic and yet the most challenging aspect of the merchant's role. The assortment is a starting point for much of the work encountered by a buyer throughout the life cycle management of the products. Forecasting and replenishment begin with the assortment decisions. Ad planning is derived from the assortment. Transition, returns, store signage, and many other aspects of the business begin with the assortment.

Think of assortment management as the way a buyer translates merchandise strategies into the actual SKUs that will bring them to life. It's a very complex process. The challenge of developing an assortment lies in the vast amount of input required to make decisions and the fact that many other constituencies have a voice in the process. The inventory team, for example, lobbies for vendors that ship complete orders on time. The consumer-brand people want strong brands in the mix. Of course, gross margin is a concern. Your sourcing group wants more private label. Depending on the size of the organization, the buyer will hear from multiple areas, each concerned with their view of the business. In the end, the merchant must synthesize and consider all of the input while delivering a logical, sensible assortment that will drive the business and meet the goals.

Not surprisingly, you cannot make everyone happy. The leading brand may come from a vendor with poor shipping performance. The highest margin products may be slow sellers. The vendor with the best on time / right quantity performance may be slow to market with the new products. When the assortment is finalized, the buyer will be a hero to some, yet a villain to others.

Explaining the challenge of building or planning an assortment seemed like a daunting task. Clearly, the best way to understand it is to do it. Find a well-seasoned buyer and live through the process. To explain what the merchant encounters, I thought it best to break the explanation into parts, which will define the basic steps taken, the considerations needed, a practical example, and, lastly, some commentary or additional thoughts.

KEY STEPS

The complexity of any assortment process will vary according to the business, perhaps even the classes of merchandise within a business. In a pet superstore, the approach to dog food versus live pets will obviously vary. If a buyer is assorting file cabinets for an office products store, he'll consider letter/legal, 2-drawer/4-drawer, 25" deep / 28.5" deep, black or beige, thumb latch lock / no lock, etc. File cabinets are generally less complex than televisions. The following *steps* are general in nature, not applicable in all situations, and can change in their order.

- Collect and review strategic data
  - Industry information and trend
  - Consumer insights
  - Supplier trend information

- Shop competition

- Analyze vendor performance

- Analyze price point data

- Analyze attribute data
  - SKU level
  - Basket level

+ Rank the current assortment by revenue, unit sales, gross margin

+ Identify SKUs to drop—vendor discontinued, doesn't meet strategy, poor sales

+ Identify new items available for consideration

+ Determine new items

+ Review assortment against space considerations

+ Finalize assortment

+ Transition/exit plan for old SKU

+ Communicate to internal constituencies

ASSORTMENT CONSIDERATION

Portfolio Role and Intent—Role and intent are key inputs to category-level strategy. If assortment, as a resource lever, is important to the strategic direction or plan for a category, it may drive the addition or deletion of SKUs. For example, if your intent is to "optimize" a product category, it probably means reducing the number of SKUs offered. A "grow" intent might drive the expansion of the category.

Supply Chain Performance Metrics—A review of each vendor's shipping performance is always good preparation. A vendor that ships incomplete orders, is chronically late, or fails to meet your standards is probably not a vendor whose business you want to grow by adding SKUs. A poor on-time/ right quantity (OTRQ) performance will directly translate into lost sales. It doesn't matter how great the deal was if the goods aren't available for sale. If the vendor's shipments are unreliable, you will lose. Many companies monitor and track vendor performance. As you approach the assortment process, it's helpful to know key performance indicators. Does the vendor ship on time? Are orders complete (the constant receipt of backorders is very expensive)? Does the vendor meet your compliance criteria for things like pallet size, EDI (electronic data interchange), packing list, preferred carriers, and so forth?

Space—If available, space management analytics can be very useful data. If a category is limited to twelve linear feet, a decision to add items may be mute. Conversely, the dropping of too many items may create a need to broker space to another, adjacent category.

Return Rates—This should be reviewed by product and by vendor. High returns can be a silent killer of your business that is often hidden. Aside from the customer satisfaction issues, returns are very costly even if the vendor provides full credit.

Ad Strategy—Is this category advertised? Are there company-wide events that must be supported? Many drug chains, as an example, will run Dollar Days or Buy One Get One (BOGO) Free ads. As a buyer of frames, tape, film, or other participating categories, you would account for these events when planning the assortment. A 5 x 7 frame may be assorted solely so that you can promote it quarterly in a 1 cent sale or BOGO event.

Category and Brand Strategy—What's my strategy for the category? Does a good-better-best selection make sense? Is private label an opportunity or are national brands exclusively needed? A strategy of being the low-price leaders will lead to select brands and SKUs. If the strategy is to be the authority, the depth of an assortment would be much deeper.

External Market Intelligence—Often, industry sources or suppliers can provide research on trends that help position an assortment. In 2006, the actual rounds of golf played in the United States declined

3.6 percent. If you're managing the assortment for golf equipment, this is a fact worth noting. Forecasts for new technology can be very significant. Years ago, every desk in America had a 4 x 6 memo pad holder on it. Then 3M invented Post-it notes. Paper merchants saw a profound effect on their assortments. During the shift from analog to digital technology, electronics retailers and mass retailers constantly sought industry data or manufacturing forecasts on the trends. How many analog televisions versus digital? When will 35 mm cameras stop selling and be replaced by digital? When will the digital trend move to digital SLR?

Solution or the experience—Many items make it into an assortment because there is a need to complete a solution or a purchase experience. Examples might be replacement batteries for a cordless phone or watch or pipe cleaners in a craft assortment.

Back-end Programs—When creating an assortment, it is imperative that the buyer know the true landed cost of products. I have seen many examples of merchants choosing SKU XYZ because the gross margin was 5 percent higher than a competitor's offer only to discover that the competition had a 10 percent volume allowance that actually made their product 5 percent less expensive. Know your vendor programs!

Vendor Rationalization—If only one or two items are purchased from a specific vendor, does it make sense to do business with them? There are costs associated with maintenance, purchase orders, receiving the goods, meeting with the supplier, and more. Is it worth it? Consider moving these items to another supplier where you can build volume and be a more meaningful customer.

This list of considerations is certainly not exhaustive, but it provides a sense of how complex the assortment creation process can be. The buyer must receive, analyze, and act on many points of view, many data points and insights. As a way to make the process more realistic, the following fictitious view of a digital camera assortment was created. Take a close look at the following charts.

Camera Assortment by Price Point

Vendor	SKU	Retail	Units Sold	GM
Aries	Camera 1	$89	900	25%
Libra	Camera 2	$99	3,400	19%
Capricorn	Camera 3	$99	1,800	20%
Aries	Camera 4	$129	300	25%
Taurus	Camera 5	$129	400	18%
Gemini	Camera 6	$149	3,160	19%
Pisces	Camera 7	$149	461	22%
Virgo	Camera 8	$149	3,700	19%
Capricorn	Camera 9	$199	5,460	20%
Gemini	Camera 10	$199	6,000	20%
Aries	Camera 11	$199	5,200	20%
Virgo	Camera 12	$199	5,000	19%
Libra Pixie	Camera 13	$224	2,900	20%
Pisces	Camera 14	$229	314	26%
Taurus	Camera 15	$229	608	18%
Capricorn	Camera 16	$279	4,100	21%
Capricorn	Camera 17	$299	621	20%
Gemini	Camera 18	$299	529	20%
Virgo	Camera 19	$299	1,510	20%
Libra Pixie	Camera 20	$299	3,700	20%
Libra	Camera 21	$299	1,600	20%
Libra	Camera 22	$319	110	21%
Pisces	Camera 23	$349	270	26%
Virgo	Camera 24	$379	1,900	20%
Libra	Camera 25	$399	2,300	20%
Capricorn	Camera 26	$399	540	20%
Libra	Camera 27	$449	800	21%
Virgo	Camera 28	$499	1,500	22%
Gemini SLR	Camera 29	$699	800	14%
Libra Shooter	Camera 30	$799	2,000	13%
Gemini SLR	Camera 31	$799	400	17%
Libra SLR	Camera 32	$899	906	14%
Virgo SLR	Camera 33	$899	227	14%
Gemini SLR	Camera 34	$1,299	90	18%

Vendor by Price Point

Libra	Virgo	Capricorn	Taurus
$99	$149	$99	$129
$224	$199	$199	$229
$299	$299	$279	
$299	$379	$299	
$319	$499	$399	
$399	$899 SLR		
$449 SLR			
$799 SLR			
$899 SLR			
(9)	(6)	(5)	(2)
Aries	Pisces	Gemini	
$89	$149	$149	
$129	$229	$199	
$199	$349	$299	
		$699 SLR	
		$799 SLR	
		$1,299 SLR	
(3)	(3)	(6)	Total (34)

Vendor Performance

	# SKUs	GM	OTRQ	Returns	Payment Terms	Back-end Allowances
Libra	9	21	76%	9%	N60	6%
Pisces	3	26	80%	31%	N45	2%
Capricorn	5	23	91%	12%	N60	6%
Gemini	6	20	89%	7%	N60	5%
Aries	3	25	70%	24%	N60	8%

Virgo	6	19	65%	9%	N45	3%
Taurus	3	18	67%	15%	N30	2%

The charts offer no real item information, and all of the data are purely fictitious. Still, it can serve/provide insights into the assortment thought process through observation.

OBSERVATIONS

1. The assortment by price points offers a quick glance at SKU performance and which price points are most effective. Many companies or buyers will do a price band analysis to understand what customers are willing to pay. At a glance, it's obvious that $199 is the primary price band (over 20,000 units sold).

2. More cameras are sold at the $199 price point than then at $99. This indicates that consumers want more featured products, not cheap cameras.

3. The Libra Shooter jumps out as the top selling DSLR (digital single-lens reflex) camera. It's also the lowest gross margin SKU in the mix.

4. Libra dominates the DSLR business. Virgo is "suspect." With low sales and low gross margin, why is this item in the mix? Note it as an opportunity for replacement or a leverage issue to gain more gross margin. You'd be surprised how much margin can be gained when the facts say "drop the SKU."

5. The Vendor by Price Point chart will generate some thought.

   a. Libra has three SKUs at $299 or $319. Is there enough differentiation? At $299, the Pixie is a sleek, more compact camera than the other Libra cameras. Three units this close in price, however, probably isn't sensible.

b. Taurus has only two SKUs in the offering and neither one is a gang buster item. If other vendors are fighting to break in, this may be an opportunity.

c. Pisces and Aries are worth a hard look. What's the purpose or role for each? Pisces sales are weak. Aries is better and provides that OPP (opening price point) of $89 that can be an image driver.

d. Capricorn seems balanced with good steps.

e. Gemini seems balanced with good steps. If other factors are positive, this may be a vendor to add SKUs with. There's a gap between $299 and $699.

6. The Vendor Performance chart adds more insight.

a. Taurus is low on gross margin, poor on shipping performance, has the lowest back-end support, and has terms that are well-below average. With vendors like Scorpio, Leo, and Sagittarius wanting to come in, I'd drop the vendor quickly.

b. Returns of Aries cameras are much too high. Performance is subpar. The opportunity to replace this vendor or consolidate SKUs is great.

c. Pisces is below the bar on payment terms, back-end support, and their return rate is far too high. Pisces does offer a complete solution with computer and photo printers. Here, the merchant must weigh the strategic importance of keeping Pisces in the assortment against the probability of improving the metrics and the programs.

d. Libra is performing well. The slightly lower gross margin is driven by sales of the Shooter SLR. They may be a candidate to pick up more business. As the buyer approaches a negotiation with Libra, additional business needs to be earned with some improvement to gross margin or the back end.

e. Libra, Gemini, Capricorn, and Virgo emerge as the core of the business. Each has areas for improvement,

but overall, a balanced assortment between them may
be healthy and keep each eager to earn more.

Another way to cut the data when preparing an assortment is by feature. Many buyers will create a feature list and plot the SKUs with sales, gross margin, returns, and more against it. In the camera example, a feature slice at the assortment might include mega pixels, screen/viewer size, optical zoom, and so forth. A binder assortment might be viewed as standard, D-ring, view binders, and locking. Dog food might break down into wet, dry, puppy, adult, and senior. Essentially, any product grouping has feature sets that can be viewed to understand the contribution to sales. The results might be a SKU reduction in the slow-selling features while bolstering the growth areas.

The point is that the merchant needs to bring multiple data sources and considerations to bear when reviewing and planning an assortment. I have yet to see a tool or system that can do the work. So this work remains more art than science.

Some Extras on Assortment

Static Assortments

Not all categories of merchandise are as dynamic as electronics. An office products buyer of paper clips would be more focused on sales and gross margin. After an assortment is in place (standard/jumbo, metal/plastic), they don't change a lot. Yes, portfolio comes into play, and innovation does occur; but let's face it, it's less dynamic than an iPod.

Market-tailored Assortments

Often, large chains will tailor assortment to local markets. A Kroger in Texas will have much more Mexican food than a Kroger in Illinois. Target stores in Florida don't offer snow scrapers. While some of those decisions are obvious, many are more subtle. Canary legal pads outsell white 4:1 in Northern states. Gas appliances don't sell in many parts of Florida (there is no gas). Big button telephones sell well in Arizona, Florida, and the Ozarks (retirees).

Today, there are sophisticated tools that can analyze sales and cluster products as unique assortments. The result is that stores can maximize efficiency and space to improve sales and customer satisfaction.

Strategy

I once reviewed an assortment of car stereo products and noticed that only two SKUs were purchased from AIWA—neither was a key item. The buyer explained that all vendors use MAP (minimum advertised price) policies to keep everyone even competitively. AIWA was a vendor he used to promote at key times, knowing he could break MAP and get away with it. It fit his category strategy.

This is just one example. Is being a price leader on the opening price point a part of the strategy? Are trade-ups (good/better/best) important? Where does private label fit? What brands are important and what brand positioning is needed (basic, mainstream, premium, super premium)? Gas stations masterfully slipped in a midoctane that nobody really needs. It created a "good-better-best" scenario, claimed about 15 percent of sales, and improved their average ticket and gross margin. Strategy is a key to good assortment work.

Vendor-managed Assortments

Many product categories are either driven by the supplier or too SKU intensive for a buyer to manage. In grocery and drug channels, vendor managed assortments are referred to as DSD (direct store delivery). Cookies, crackers, and snack foods fall into this classification. The merchant actually brokers the store space (12 feet of cookies, 24 feet of salty snacks, etc.), and the vendor will merchandise the space to maximize sales. An example of SKU intensive category might be greeting cards. The buyer doesn't review and select each card. Rather, they select a vendor and broker the space.

Narrow and Deep

This term is often used to describe an assortment plan that has limited breath of choice but greater variety within the chosen products. As an example, a broad assortment of copy paper might offer an opening price point, generic brand, several national brands, premium copy paper, card or index stock, all in multiple colors and sizes. A narrow and deep assortment might offer Hammermill paper only, but in 8 ½ x 11, 8 ½ x 14, 11 x 17, six colors of each, 20 lb weight, 24lb weight, by the ream, and by the case of ten.

Step-up Strategy

In many assortments, a step-up strategy or a good-better-best approach is employed as a way to enhance the average selling price (ASP) or improve margins. A basic microwave oven is offered at a competitive price of $79. A more featured microwave sells for $129 as a "step" to gain a higher sale. Many home centers will offer no name light bulbs to show an aggressive price, but also offer GE, Phillips, or Sylvania as a step-up.

Good/better/best is similar. As an example, a home improvement store may offer a basic paint (five-year warranty), a stepup (ten-year warranty), and a premium (twenty-year warranty). Most office products stores apply this strategy in multiple categories. A basic 8 ½ x 11 binder at a price is offered in a 1" size, black only. The "better" binders come in 1/2", 1", 1 ½", 2", and 3". Multiple colors are offered as well. The "best" binder may be D-ring or locking binders.

Private Label

When Office Depot opened their first stores in Florida, a little known stationary store named Jaffe's found it hard to compete. Large discounts on national brands squeezed margins. An element of their assortment strategy was to place a private label next to key national brands. This offered a better value to the consumer, a much greater margin for Jaffe's, and they remained competitive on the national brands. The consumer found Jaffe's brand correction fluid (more for less) next to Liquid Paper, Jaffe's brand cellophane tape next to 3M Scotch Magic Tape 810, a dozen Jaffe's brand stick pens next to Paper Mate Write Bros. pens, and so forth. The strategy worked splendidly.

Transitions

Assortment planning and transition go hand in hand. Transition is the plan that gets new items onto the shelf and old items out of the stores. In a perfect world, the last piece of a discontinued SKU would sell on the day the new or replacement SKU arrives in the store. Of course, retail is not perfect.

Retailers deal with this challenge in a variety of ways. In soft lines, clearance racks are positioned in aisles or within department traffic patterns to create excitement and to move the goods out. Progressive markdowns are normal (25% off, followed by 50% off, even 75% off) because the goods must go to make way for the next season. In hard lines categories, you may find specific space or fixtures dedicated to clearance product. Some retailers will advertise clearance specials. Some will sell goods to a third party at a loss just to get them out of the stores. An entire subculture exists within retail around closeout and clearance merchandise.

Having seen good and having seen bad, I believe the most critical activity that can occur to make transitions smooth is simply communication. The buyer must let the appropriate people know what SKUs are going away and what SKUs are coming in with as much advanced notice as is possible.

Customer Focus

Buyers that select products based on their personal preferences are doomed to failure. A merchant needs to know the marketplace and know the consumer.

Don't Over Assort

Many years ago, I took the helm of the furniture department in an office products superstore. I quickly noticed that we offered 125 chairs in our seating assortment, and sales had been flat or declining for two years. With some analysis, I discovered that the root cause of the problem was that we were over assorted. The company had financial goals in place and prudently limited purchasing with an open-to-buy amount. In the chair category, the lackluster sales performance limited the open-to-buy dollars to the degree that each chair had essentially one "to show" and only one or two "to go." A chair sold on Tuesday was often out of stock until the next week. Additionally, 40-50 percent of my inventory was tied up in display. I quickly reduced SKUs. Within ninety days, an assortment of 75 chairs was producing a 30 percent sales increase. Lesson learned—don't over assort.

Lastly, assortment management is very much about making decisions, and this critical piece will often separate the good buyers from the mediocre ones. While there is some science on the input side, this is still mostly a process of "art" and of making a deal. There are always more possibilities than there is space or dollars. That means, the buyer must say no to someone. I will always urge merchants to make fact-based decisions, but what's even more critical—just make a decision. Too often I've seen buyers ask a vendor for more information or tell a vendor, "I'll get back to you," when the reality is just the simple struggle to make a decision. More than once I've heard the cry from a vendor, "Tell me yes, tell me no. Just tell me something."

Chapter Five

ALLOWANCES

R etail is detail. I don't know who first used that phrase, but I do know that there is a lot of truth in it. I can think of no aspect of the merchant's responsibilities that more requires attention to detail than allowances. I also know, from firsthand experience, that poorly managed allowance programs can cost a company a lot of profit. In 1997, PharMor declared Chapter 11 bankruptcy. As hordes of auditors and consultants scrutinized financial records, they discovered that allowance management and collection was something of a black hole into which millions of dollars were lost each year.

All major retailers employ post-audit groups. The sole mission for these people is to unearth lost monies and gather documentation to go back and collect it. The vast majority of these collections are directly related to allowances. In fact, the challenge is so pervasive that many national chains employ several groups to search for lost monies. Often, there is an internal department, which is augmented by one or two outside agencies. The outside firms are paid a percentage of what they collect as "lost" money, and I assure you, they all make a very nice living off of retailers (reference section on "Post-audit Claims").

So, why is this so complicated? I have studied this topic in at least half a dozen companies and the learnings are similar in all of them. First, there's an issue of language. Almost every retailer touches multiple industries. For example, the clothing industry, the beauty care industry, the music industry, greeting cards, beverage, candy, housewares, and more are all found within a Target store. Cosmetics, pharmacy, magazines, film, tobacco, and school supplies can be found in a Rite Aid or Walgreens. Even specialty retailers touch multiple industries (a Best Buy carries furniture, music, movies, computers, and consumer electronics).

Different industries have different "speak" around allowances. The term "post off," as an example, is unique to alcoholic beverages. "Trailing Credit" is not a common term, but the vacuum-cleaner manufacturers use it regularly. Co-op, MDF (Market Development Funds), advertising, rebate, accrual, off invoice, bill back, incentive, free goods, and on and on. Often, the same words may have a different meaning, depending on the industry. So language is the first challenge.

Math is another problem. The method of calculating an allowance may differ from one manufacturer to another or between the retailer and the supplier. This is further explained later in this chapter when "Absolute Gross Margin" is addressed.

Documentation is another culprit. Allowances need to be clearly defined and documented. This complication is especially significant here because allowances often touch multiple departments. The buyer negotiates the allowance. They hand off to a specialist. The specialist sets up an entry into the ledger as a receivable. The account payables department sees the "off invoice" allowances. Are you getting the picture?

My approach has always been to simplify allowances by breaking the topic into several digestible pieces. These include a basic description of the types of allowances, the manner in which allowances are received, some universal definitions or descriptions of allowances, a checkbook concept for controlling allowances, a description of absolute gross margin, and some general filler on the topic. Like most parts of this work, grasping these fundamentals will provide a framework from which any variation can be understood and dealt with. Additionally, I have delivered this approach to numerous groups and have met with success each time because the concepts are foundational and the terms fairly universal across most industries.

Definitions and How Allowances Are Received

Before reading further, familiarize yourself with the chart labeled "Allowances." I created this simple view of allowances over twenty years ago, and it still holds true today. Reference it as needed.

An allowance is, by definition, an incentive. It is offered or provided to reward, support, or encourage some action by the recipient. The chart labeled "Allowances" is a graphic depiction of how to think about allowances. Allowances are classified in one of six buckets: use of money, cooperative advertising, accrued types of allowances, MDF/promotional allowances, price protection, or miscellaneous. In general ledger systems, these allowances are accounted for as a reduction to the expense of advertising (either in general or a reduction to a specific ad event) or the cost of goods (an improvement to gross margin).

The chart also notes how allowances are received. Some come as a percentage off invoice. Some allowances are accrued and rebated monthly, quarterly, or even yearly. Often, a vendor will offer free goods as payment. The bottom line, and one of the things that makes this topic so confusing, is that there is almost an infinite number of combinations of allowances and how they are collected.

Allowances

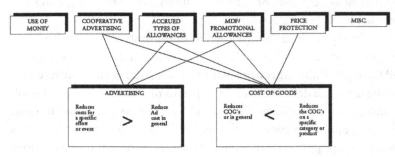

How Allowances Are Received

PERCENT OFF INVOICE	REBATES - goods sold - goods purchased	FREE GOODS	SPECIAL COST, QUOTED PRICE, TRAILING CREDIT

How Allowances Are Defined, Claimed, and Collected

Net Purchases Gross purchases minus returns, minus price protection, if applicable. When giving a promotional allowance, returns and price protections should be the only factors in determining net purchases. Before negotiating any allowances, the purchase price should be determined, and then the negotiating should begin.

Payment Terms Often a "Use of Money" allowance. For example, 2%10NET30 is an offer of a 2% discount or allowance if the invoice is paid within 10 days. The vendor is providing an incentive for early payment. It's not really different than a bank offering a free toaster when you open an account. It's a reward for using your money.

Payment terms are taken by the accounts payables group within a retail organization. Although the discounts seldom credit a buyer's gross-margin performance, they are an advantage to the company. Think big picture.

Cooperative Advertising (Co-op) Most vendors offer some program to support the consumer advertising of a retailer. Most typically, this is an allowance that is accrued and paid monthly (MBB stands for monthly bill back) or quarterly (QBB stands for quarterly bill back) and credits the ad expense of a company.

Some notes:

1. Co-op is a promotional advertising allowance based on a percentage of net purchases.
2. All co-op negotiated as DFI (Deducted from Invoice) is collected by the payables department. Many retailers will take this as a reduction to the cost of goods because it's off invoice. Caution: know your real gross margin.
3. If co-op is accrued, it is most commonly paid by issuing a credit memo or a vendor may pay by check. Free goods is an option that should be discouraged. (More on this later.)

4. If a vendor requires proof of performance, it means that, typically, tear sheets (copies of the ad) are submitted with the claim. In extreme circumstances, some vendors may require documentation proving the actual cost of that particular ad (printer invoices, invoices from all newspapers, and measurements detailing their exact space). This proof of performance should be discouraged. This requires an enormous degree of paperwork to collect.

5. Some vendors have very specific rules associated with their co-op programs. Intel, for example, has numerous rules on the use of their logo. A buyer needs to know the rules or a lost allowance may result.

Accrued Types of Allowances

Accrued simply means that they build over time and are tied to volume. A "2% quarterly bill back" means that each quarter the retailer may claim 2% of the purchases made in that quarter as a chargeback to the vendor. These allowances can be for volumes, returns, freight or any number of activities. As seen by the lines on the chart, these allowances may reduce ad costs or the cost of goods. Again, it's important to clarify the intent of any allowance. A reduction in the cost of goods will impact gross margin. Ad costs are typically found elsewhere in a P and L.

Market Development Funds (MDF)

This is a percentage of net purchases or a specified dollar amount for a particular event. Most vendors retain MDF for use in building their business or taking advantage of unique opportunities. Typically, these allowances are negotiated on a case-by-case basis.

If a retailer does a television campaign, as an example, the buyer might seek funds above and beyond the normal program. If a vendor wants extraordinary exposure to introduce a new product, they may offer MDF to buy additional space with the retailer.

MDF can be a way for a manufacturer to support many different ways of increasing their sales because it is essentially money earmarked for development. A buyer can negotiate MDF for store placement of products (end caps, check lanes), financing offers, newspaper ads, Internet exposure, just about anything.

Because this type of allowance stands outside of a standard program, the merchant must always document the agreement. Most retailers have internal forms to capture MDF. Always have the form signed or get the deal in writing.

Price Protection In this circumstance, dollars are provided by the supplier to bolster a retailer's gross margin. Suppose a supplier and retailer work together to introduce a new product. The product retails for $9.99 and costs $6.00 (a gross margin of 40%). Once in the marketplace, the product doesn't sell, and a price reduction or markdown is needed. If the price were dropped to $7.99, the retailer would need a cost of $4.79 in order to retain a 40GM. A price protection would be $1.21 (difference between original of $6.00 cost and $4.79) multiplied by the number of units in stock.

This credit would be applied to the cost of goods in order to keep the margin whole. It's a common practice in retail.

Volume Rebates Volume rebates, often referred to as a VIR (Volume Incentive Rebate), are a vendor's way of pushing a retailer to do more business or promote their products in order to attain a volume level made attractive by an incentive. Typically, these types of allowances are afforded the retailer in one of two ways:

1. A Straight VIR. Make one million dollars in purchases and receive a 2% rebate. As is true of all allowances, a buyer should thoroughly understand the specifics of a volume incentive. Is the allowance based on gross

purchases? Net purchases after returns? Is it rebated yearly? Can it be taken quarterly? Remember, retail is detail!

2. A Progressive Incentive. Do $1 million in volume and earn a 1% rebate; do $2 million and earn 2%; do $2.5 million and earn 3%. Volume incentives are most often considered a reduction to the cost of goods. A buyer may factor this into calculating gross margin. The caution here is to estimate anticipated volume and don't plan on 3% back unless the $2.5 million is a slam dunk.

I have witnessed many circumstances of a margin shortfall due to poor planning around volume rebates. The $2.5 million, for example, seems like a sure thing, but the buyer drops the top 2 performing SKUs midway through the year. Oops, the 3% advantage turned into 1%.

I have also seen targets missed because of factory problems where the vendor backorders products. If the supplier is at fault, the buyer should push his/her claim for the full allowance.

Some notes:

a. Always determine if the allowance is applicable to the incremental volume or on all purchases back to dollar one.

b. When changing suppliers, volume incentives are often lost. Which is better, a cost of $1.00 or a cost of $1.02 with a 5% volume rebate? Always be sure to compare apples to apples (net cost to net cost), especially when changing suppliers.

Freight Allowances

Freight terms are another significant factor of profitability, and allowances often come into play. All major retailers have a traffic department. It is their responsibility to move goods in the most efficient manner and to negotiate favorable carrier rates.

Many retailers instruct their buyers to negotiate their products as "prepaid." That is, the cost is a landed (delivered) cost. A traffic expert may then work with the supplier to take control of the freight and negotiate an allowance in place of the vendor's costs. For example, negotiate a 5% freight allowance. If your home team can move the goods for 3 or 4%, you're ahead of the game. In other circumstances, a manufacturer may ship "FOB origin" or "FOB factory." This signifies that the retailer takes possession/ownership of the goods when they leave the factory. Often, an allowance for freight is then factored into your program.

New Store Opening or Grand Opening Allowances   The opening of a new store is a very expensive, capital-intensive proposition for a retailer. As a result, most retailers are not bashful about asking the vendor community for support. This support can be a straightforward allowance to help offset the cost, a buy-in opportunity on the initial inventory, or a very special purchasing opportunity for a grand opening ad that will drive traffic and create excitement.

Some notes:

1. Look for specified dollar amounts. For example, $5,000 per store. This is simple, straightforward, and easy to collect. Percentages off opening orders, free goods, and the like can be confusing.

2. Negotiate and specify that any new store opening allowance is also applicable to remodels or relos (relocating a store).

3. Be reasonable. If your opening order for a new store is $1000, it's probably not reasonable to expect the vendor to provide a free automobile for the grand opening. I tend to think of 10% of the initial stocking order value as a minimum threshold.

ALLOWANCE RECAP

Description	Vendor	Vendor #	Payment Terms	Freight Terms	Freight Allowance	Co-op Allowance	Defective Allowance	MDF Allowance	Volume Rebate	New Store	Note
Furniture	Chair Company	999999	NET 45	Prepaid	-	3.0%	0.50%	2.0%	1.0%	$500	
Furniture	Desk Company	999999	NET 60	Collect	2.5%	3.0%	0.50%	-	2.0%	Free displays	
Furniture	File Company	999999	NET 60	PPD/$5K	-	2.0%	0.50%		2%/over $2M	$2,000	
Furniture	Table Company	999999	NET 45	PPY&Add	2.0%		0.75%	-	-	-	
Furniture	Mat Company	999999	Consignment	Prepaid	-	3.0%	0.50%	-	-	$2,000	$10K reserve available for display
Furniture	RTA Company	999999	2%10NET30	Prepaid/$10K	-	3.0%	2.0%	2.0%	2.0%	Buy1/Get 1	Volume=1% on $1M, 2% on $3M, 3% on %5M
Furniture	Lamp Company	999999	2%10EOM	Prepaid $100	-	5.0%	2.0%	-	-		New store G.O. ad on Bankers Lamp Buy One/Get One
Furniture	Accessories Company	999999	Net 90	Prepaid $100	-	3.0%	-	-	.2%	15% off	New store = 15% initial order

A Manager's Tool

It is not at all uncommon to find allowance control in a state of disarray within a retail organization. A sharp merchant or manager must take control of the issue and put structure around it or risk the loss of money falling through the cracks. A first step that I most often employ is the allowance recap (see Allowance Recap chart). This tool brings all of the programs for a department or class of merchandise together, at a glance, by vendor.

The idea behind this tool is to view, at a glance, the programs/ allowances for each vendor within a product category. Key pieces of information include payment terms, freight policy, co-op ad allowances, MDF, new store allowances, and returns. A comments area can be a good way to capture the anomalies such as trailing credits, one-time support dollars, and so forth.

To better understand the allowance recap, note the following:

1. The example is a grouping of furniture vendors. The tool can be set up by category or by buyer.
2. Freight terms are condensed to their simplest form.

   A. Prepaid: Goods are landed at the retailer. Freight is paid by the supplier and buried in the cost of goods.

B. Prepay and Add: Freight is isolated from the cost of goods. It is paid by the vendor and "added" to the invoice as a separate line item.
C. Collect: Freight is paid for and controlled by the retailer.
D. Dollar Amounts: Denotes a minimum order amount required to receive prepaid freight.

3. Notes are used to provide a more complete picture of the opportunity.

The Checkbook

The "checkbook" is another tool used by the merchant to control and forecast allowances. The concept is simple, but if properly employed, it can be a very effective way to capture and collect all negotiated dollars.

This simple log can be expanded to meet a variety of needs. For example, add a column for "control number" if your company uses a specific form for MDF tracking. Add a column for cumulative totals if you have a target or budget and need to track progress. These additional insights may be helpful:

- The log captures over and above dollars. These dollars are negotiated as beyond the standard program, typically for a specific event such as an ad, an endcap, or check-lane positioning.
- "Program" monies are the accrued allowances. The "estimate of program" line brings these dollars in to provide a full picture of the month. This is done by estimating the programs (3% quarterly allowance, 2% co-op, etc.) and applying that percentage to the cost of goods (COGS) or purchases projected for the month. If your company projects receipts, it's a better measure than COGS.

    For example, if purchases for May are estimated at $600,000 and programs are generally 3%, you can estimate $18,000 as program dollars for the month ($600,000 X .03).

- Events: This serves as your reminder of why money is promised.
- Documentation can be an internal form or a letter from the manufacturer. It should always be signed. Listing the support without documentation is fine. It's a way to keep track of commitments, and you can follow up on documentation as needed. I do, however, recommend that the required activity does not take place (don't run the ad or set the display) without signed documentation.
- The buyer will often negotiate a calendar quarter or more worth of activity and support at a time. Some merchants may even plan yearly. By keeping a rolling January-December log, all events can be captured when recapping your negotiation.

Lastly, an MDF Log or "Checkbook" can also serve as a check and balance with accounting or audit groups. Most retailers generate some reporting on collection. These can be checked against your log to ensure proper booking of the credit. I, for example, have many times found my MDF being credited to another category by accident.

MDF Log

Month: May   Category: Snacks

Date	Vendor	Event	Amount	Signed Agreement	Comments
5/7	Chip supplier	5/7 circular, ¼ page	$2,500	Y	
5/7	Cookie supplier	5/7 circular, ½ page	$5,000	Y	Sets on 5/12
5/14	Cracker supplier	Placement fee for checklanes	$2,000	Y	
5/14	Pretzel supplier	New item introduction	$2,000	Y	

5/28	Popcorn supplier	5/28 circular, front cover	$5,000	Y	
5/30	Pretzel supplier	Webpage creation	$1,500	Y	Goes live 5/1
5/30	Cake supplier	Endcap display	$2,500	Y	Donut holes package
5/30	Chip supplier	In store demo support	$1,000	Y	Demos on 5/13, 5/20

TOTAL	$21,500
Estimate of program dollars	$18,000
Projected support for May	$39,500

Absolute Gross Margin

The term "gross margin" can have multiple meanings, and it's important that a merchant understand how it's defined in order to measure and benchmark their business. The most common use of the term defines the difference between the cost of a product and the retail selling price. This can be expressed as a dollar amount or as a percentage. Defining the actual cost can be tricky. Is that invoice cost? landed cost including freight? before or after allowances?

In a more mature company, the financial wizards are often insistent on understanding the all-in or absolute gross margin at a vendor level. While each product might have a different cost to begin with, the "absolute gross margin" is a way to define the adjustment to raw costs for a particular vendor. Understanding this (I'll call it) net net cost then allows the buyer to uniformly compare true profitability by vendor.

A basic format for looking at the net absolute percentage of allowances might look like the following:

Vendor _____   Buyer _____

Fiscal Year _____

Absolute Percentage Calculator

Allowance Description	Off Invoice/ Bill Back	Absolute Percentage	Comments
Advertising/Co-op Merchandise Rebate Warehouse Returns/Defective Misc. _____ Misc. _____ Misc. _____ Misc. _____ Payment Terms			
Net cost absolute percentage (subtract from 1.00)			

The real purpose of this exercise is to clearly define how each allowance is calculated. Think in terms of $1. If an allowance of 5% exists, it is worth 5¢ on a dollar. If a second 5% allowance exists, is the math 1.00 x .05 or .95 x .05? Do you take the second allowance off of the dollar or off of 95¢? This may seem minor, but even tenths of a cent can become large amounts when purchase orders are in the tens of millions. The following charts illustrate the difference.

Example A

Absolute Percentage Calculator

Allowance Description	Off Invoice/ Bill Back	Absolute Percentage	Comments
Advertising/Co-op	10%	.10	
Merchandise Rebate	5%	.05	
Warehouse	-	-	
Returns/Defective	5%	.05	
Misc.	-	-	
Misc.	-	-	
Misc.	-	-	
Payment Terms	Net 30	N/A	
Net cost absolute percentage (subtract from 1.00)		.80	

Example B

Absolute Percentage Calculator

Allowance Description	Off Invoice/ Bill Back	Absolute Percentage	Comments
Advertising/Co-op	10%	.10	
Merchandise Rebate	5%	.045	
Warehouse	-	-	
Returns/Defective	5%	.0427	
Misc.	-	-	
Misc.	-	-	
Misc.	-	-	
Payment Terms	Net 30	N/A	
Net cost absolute percentage (subtract from 1.00)		.8125	

The net cost absolute margin in Example A is .80. That simply means that multiplying invoice cost of goods by .8 will tell you the net net cost of goods after allowances. In Example A, each allowance is taken from 1.00. That is, the 10% is worth 10¢, the 5% is worth 5¢ and the second 5% is also worth 5¢, or an absolute of 20¢. In Example B, the allowances

88 DANIEL J. MOE

are progressive and taken after the result of the prior. Here, the 10% is worth 10¢. The 5% is worth .045. The second 5% is worth .0427 (it's taken after the 10% and the .045%). The net absolute is .8125.

On an order of $10 million, this can be quite a difference. In Example A, the net cost of goods is $8 million. In Example B the net cost of goods is $8.125 million. That's a $125,000 difference! As a buyer, if you do not clearly define and agree with your vendor on the specific value of each allowance, you will either lose money or create an accounting nightmare down the road. Remember, a lack of specific clarity around allowances is a prime reason why post-audit groups make a living (see "Post Audit" in chapter 4).

Rate Cards

Most major retailers and e-tailers develop a rate card for use in offering opportunities for advertising to their vendors. The rate card can serve multiple purposes. First, it aligns everyone in the merchant group around costs and value of ad space. When buyer Jones asks for $50,000 to support one page in a circular and buyer Smith asks for $200,000 for the same space, it creates inequity and conflict. A published rate card puts everyone on the same page. Secondly, it's an opportunity for a retailer to explain the value of their program in detail. "A direct mail piece targeted at 100,000 of our best customers carrying only five offers . . ." This specifies what you're getting for the money. Vendors can then better determine the value of their participation.

A simple rate card might look like the following:

XYZ Company—Advertising Rates	
Chainwide Television (cable)	$110,000
Chainwide Radio	$100,000
Direct Mail Stuffer (100K mailing)	$ 25,000
In Store Video (1 month)	$ 10,000
In Store Radio (1 month)	$ 6000
Chainwide Circular (48M/week)	$ 300,000/page
	150,000/ ½ page
	75,000/ ¼ page
Regional Circular (6M per)	$ 20,000/page
See your buyer for details.	

From an e-tail perspective, the rate card might look like this:

ABC.com—Advertising Rates		
Low Season February through October	**Traffic Expectations**	
	Home Page Category Pages or Tabs*	3 million visitors a week 500K visitors/week
High Season November through January	**Traffic Expectations**	
	Home Page	20 million visitors/week
	Category Pages	5 million visitors/week

Rates	**Product Feature** *Low/High*	**Gift Store Link** *Low/High*	**What's New link** *Low/High*
Home Page	$15K/$30K	$5K/$10K	$5K/$10K
Category Page	$7K/$20K	$5K/$10K $	5K/$10K
Splash Page Features	$15K		

*Amazon may serve as a good example for this illustration.

The home page is tabbed with books, apparel, electronics, toys, and more.

These could be the "Category" pages.

Odds and Ends

Some notes about this topic of allowances.

1. Be realistic. There are as many wacky ideas on how to provide allowances as there are vendors. An allowance that is so complicated that it cannot be collected is almost worthless. Try this one:

Vendor provides 4% co-op to be accrued and paid quarterly. Items XYZ and QRS are exceptions. They will receive 2% co-op. In the fourth quarter, no items will receive co-op. The allowance excludes new item additions for the first 120 days after introduction. Can anyone keep track of this effectively?

OR

Vendor will give away a free horse and buggy with all purchases of $100,000 or more.

The point here: Keep it simple!

2.   Free goods. Avoid them unless there is absolutely no alternative. Vendors often like this option because it actually costs them less than real dollars. The problems, however, can quickly overwhelm you. How are free goods purchased? Received? If you order one hundred units and ten are free, what happens if only sixty are shipped? Did you get the free ones or not? Trust me. Avoid free goods at all costs.

3.   Document. Always require confirmation of any program in writing, on vendor letterhead. Be sure it's signed.

4.   Be specific. If you have 5% co-op, 5% MDF, and 5% volume, do the math with the vendor. Are all three "5s" off of $1 or is one off of $1, the second off of $.95 and the third off of $.902? Is the 5% off gross purchases or after returns? Be specific.

5.   Diligence and follow up. Allowances need to be reviewed regularly. Challenge them. Are you collecting them? Are you receiving credit in your numbers?

Lastly, I'm compelled to point out that the world could be a simpler and more cost-efficient place if allowances didn't exist. I suspect that they came into existence as a way to reward alignment to the manufacturer or to entice a retailer to buy one product line over another. However we got to the place that exists today, allowances surely complicate a merchant's life.

The world's largest retailer has recognized this and, because of their power and determination, has been very successful in educating the vendor community on the efficiency of simplified programs. The Wal-Mart or Sam's Club merchant drives to understand true cost of a product. Forget about MDF, freight, the company golf tournament, and all the other factors that hide true net cost. If the merchant can get to the lowest common denominator and run their business efficiently, there are many additional savings to be had and greater benefit to the end consumer. By reducing or eliminating all the paperwork, follow up, payroll, and time needed to manage and collect allowances, a retailer can put a lot more to the bottom line.

Chapter Six

POST-AUDIT CLAIMS

Literally translated, the term "Post-audit Claim" refers to a claim (charge back to the vendor) which is generated as the result of an audit. All major retailers either have a post-audit claim group of their own or they contract with an external company to do this work. In fact, many retailers will employ more than one team. I know of several large retailers that employ as many as three post-audit teams. One is an internal group. Two are external.

The basic purpose or mission of these teams is to audit agreements, contracts, documentation, and terms to be sure that the retailer collected everything that was due him. They search accounting systems. They will work with merchant groups to review their files and records. They dig into freight bills, advertising, and purchasing records as they hunt for the promise that wasn't met or the deal that may have slipped through the cracks. When an error is found, the auditor will write up a claim and usually ask that the merchant or other responsible party review the claim and sign off on its legitimacy before a deduction is made against a vendor.

External groups are paid a percentage of what they identify and is actually collected by the company. They make a good living.

The cost of post-audit claims to a company is measured in two ways. First, there is the expense of the fees paid to the auditing group(s). Although this cost may vary between audit groups and retailers, a general rule of thumb is that 15-30% of what is recovered goes to the audit team. A second factor is the cost of capital. If your company has been without the dollars in the bank, you have certainly lost the interest value of those dollars. As an example of the total cost associated with post-audit recovered dollars, lets assume that the commission rate paid to the external post-audit group is 20%. During my last year at PharMor, the external group recovered approximately $25.4 million.

- Approximately $5.1 million was paid in commission to the post-audit group ($25.4 million recovered X 20%).
- The average time between the actual original transaction and the collection through post audit is eighteen months. At a cost of capital of 11%, that's an additional $4.2 million ($25.4 M X 11% X 18 mos.) lost to the company.
- Total loss in this example was $9.3 million.

While some retailers may attempt to charge back the lost capital cost, the fact is they failed to claim it. The vendor did not fail to pay it.

Examples of Post-audit Claims

Claim #A-1234   Jones Corporation $4,512 Invoice Pricing Error
Jones Corporation reduced the price on model #XL910 effective January 1, 1999. Subsequent to that date, five invoices were billed and paid at the old higher cost. This claim recovers that cost difference.

Claim #B-2345   Acme Corporation $27,515 Volume Rebate
Acme offered a .5% rebate for the achievement of a specified level of volume and an additional .5% rebate for the achievement of a second tier of volume. Research indicates that we achieved both levels of volume but never claimed or received the rebates.

Claim #C-3456   Presto Co. $50,000 Promo Funding
Presto offered a $100,000 incentive for the purchase of twenty thousand units of item XYZ. Research indicates that orders were placed for more that twenty thousand units. Presto, however, back ordered ten thousand pieces and, therefore, only paid half of the incentive. We believe the additional $50,000 is due as we met our terms of the agreement.

Claim #D-5678   Federal Sales Co. $22,560 Trailing Credit
Federal Sales offered a $21.50 trailing credit for each model 777 purchased between April 1 and October 31. Our company has not submitted a claim for this credit, nor has credit been issued.

Claim #E-6789   United Sales $12,680 New Item Credit
United offers this company a 10% off allowance on the initial purchase of all new items. Research indicates that two new items were added (item QRS and item TUV), for which the allowance was never claimed.

Claim #A-4321   Acme Sales $6,982 Return Freight
Acme's return policy states that they will pay the freight back on all returns. During the period of February 15 through September 30, there were six product returns made with freight prepaid. The claim is to recoup that freight.

Claim #B-8765   American Candy Co. $28,000 Invoice Pricing
American agreed to sell our company lollipops at $61.50 per case ($4 below-standard cost). Seven thousand cases were ordered, yet we were billed at the higher cost.

Claim #C-9876   Belmont Co. $36,000 Price Protection
Belmont lowered the cost of model 9999 by $2 effective May 1. They agreed to price protect all inventory (eighteen thousand units). No record of payment can be found, nor did we claim this price protection.

Again, these claims generally require someone's review and approval before they are filed with the vendor. This "approval" is important. Remember, the post-audit group is paid on what is collected. They generate a lot of energy and zeal around their claims. The merchant or business person that authorizes the claim may not want to go after money that's five or six years old and jeopardize the relationship. Or they may know that vendor XYZ helped with some other deal or expense in lieu of a particular issue. Be sure to review all claims before signing off and launching a vendor charge back.

Reducing Post-audit Claims

Post-audit claims are like mini-mysteries that simply need some good detective work to solve. Often, that detective work is not addressed. There's a claim here and a claim there. As a merchandising executive, I might see five claims one day and then none for two months. There are always more important activities to get after than drilling down to the root cause of these charge backs. That's why the auditor makes a good living.

Twice in my life, the bombardment of post-audit claims hit me hard enough that I invested the time necessary to get to the root cause. The activity can be summarized in four steps.

1. Capture and aggregate claims
    I began by contacting each post-audit group (these were three separate groups when I last did this) and verified that my departments would process no claim unless I specifically signed the claim. This ensured that I would see all claims and backup materials. I logged these in the following manner (a fictitious example):

Date	Dept.	Vendor	Amount	Reason
5/15	Seasonal	Atico	$19,000	Price protection
5/22	Picture Frames	Acme	$34,000	New item allowance
5/22	Greeting Cards	Novo	$21,000	Failed to claim 2% DFI
6/9	Gift Wrap	Cleo	$8,000	Volume rebate
6/9	Photo Albums	MBI	$9,421	Promo cost not taken
6/16	Gift Wrap	Cleo	$14,020	Vendor billing error
6/21	Seasonal	Atico	$6,500	Promo cost

2. Analyze claims to determine root cause
    Typically, back-up material for any claim is readily available. It explains the logic or reason for the claim and contains the research and documentation unearthed by the post-audit group. While the review is tedious, often boring work, I found that about 25% of the time, I rejected the claims. The remaining valid claims I would categorize as in the above "reason" columns.

3. Analyze results

By recapping the claims, I had a simplified view of the landscape over a specific period of time. This allowed for grouping like claims, slicing the list by vendor, essentially looking for the patterns.

Do any vendors appear most often?
Can "reasons" for the claims be grouped?
Is any particular category (or buyer) more prone to claims?

For example:

Total Claims:	44	By Reason
Reasons		
Promo Cost	11	25%
New Store Allowance	8	18%
New Item Allowance	6	14%
Volume Rebate Missed	5	11%
Other	14	32%

This view quickly points out that 57% of the problems can be isolated to promo cost issues or allowances for new stores and new items. When sliced by vendor or by buyer, the data may reveal a similar pattern.

4. Recommended Actions

Once the reasons for post-audit claims have been identified and grouped, it becomes easier to develop an action plan to address the root causes. For example, I found that a key gap existed in training merchants about allowances and vendor setup. Merchants thought the inventory team would address promo costs through the purchase orders. The inventory team assumed the merchants were claiming it. Once we trained people and clearly identified roles and responsibilities we virtually eliminated the "Promo Cost" issue or 25% of the claims.

Other recommendations from the above analysis:

- Revise the vendor setup forms. The form in use did not provide a clear, specific definition for allowances.
- Create a training that explains how to document and claim allowances (volume rebates, new store, etc.).

In Closing

The topic of allowances and claims is possibly the most complicated arena within business. The post-audit function is charged with the financial recovery of substantial amounts of money. While the practice is extremely valuable, it also serves as a vivid reminder of the gaps that allow dollars to slip through the cracks of any organization. Therefore, in addition to financial recovery, any post-audit group must be charged with developing educational programs that can eliminate future claims by filling the gaps before the errors occur.

Operating efficiently is the best win for your company and for the vendor.

Chapter Seven

BUILDING AN AD PLAN

One of the most time consuming and critical activities of the merchant is promotional planning. The creation of advertising (newspaper, Sunday circulars, radio, TV, direct mail) is a complex process with multiple touch points. Typically, a marketing group or management will set strategy and direction for the company. The merchant may be a participant, but his task really begins when the details of a marketing plan are provided. For example, someone or some group will determine that the company will use a Sunday circular. The circular will be twenty-four pages or thirty-two pages. The company will direct mail to known customers weekly, and so forth.

Given the framework in which to work, the merchant role is to marry the appropriate products, brands, prices, and promotions to the plan and move the information to the production people. The production side will typically assist with creative, layout, printing, and circulation. Thus, the merchant finds himself responsible for making the ad come to life . . . taking direction on one end and providing direction to the other. As the "cradle to grave" owner of the product, if there's no stock for the ad, a wrong picture appears, or a price is in error, the buyer is ultimately the responsible party.

In order to explain this complicated activity, I've broken down the subject into four broad topics: the purpose of an ad plan, basic data and information needed, the tools used, and issues for consideration or thought. Additionally, these learnings center on a mainstream retail organization, which typically does print advertising. The fundamentals and principles, however, can be applied to most situations.

Purpose of an Ad Plan

A former mentor of mine was fond of saying, "If you don't know where you're going, any road will take you there." An ad plan is a progression of the category strategy and provides the direction needed to meet objectives. When done correctly, it allows an ease of execution for the buyer and the teams that interface. A good plan for advertising can also prepare the merchant for negotiating. A prepared merchant uses an agenda for his vendor meetings, and prethinking the category advertising will help frame up what to discuss. For example, a *One Cent* sale event may be planned for Memorial Day. Or a *Buy One, Get One* sale (BOGO—buy one four-pack of AA batteries, get the second free) may be in the plan. Advanced planning and knowledge of such events will frame up the discussion of vendor support.

Planning also means documenting. Many years ago, I happened into a restaurant in Youngstown, Ohio, and was seated in a booth next to two sales reps. At the time, I had just started working for PharMor, and these gentlemen had just finished a sales call. It seems that they had just closed a big deal on some housewares. I overheard one say to the other, "Good lord, John. You just about gave away the store in there. Fifty thousand dollars and a five percent rebate is far too rich." To which John replied, "Don't worry about it. These guys love to negotiate, but three months from now, no one will collect it. That buyer will have been moved to a different category, and he never asks for documentation. They've only collected about half of what we offered up last year." Moral of the story: document, document, document.

Ad planning has additional benefit. From an inventory perspective, it allows the team to meet stock requirements and avoid customer disappointments. In retail, it's considered a mortal sin to be out of stock on an ad item. By having a solid plan done according to an appropriate timeline in stock problems can be mitigated. Conversely, I have all too often seen buyers who look to serve up the ad candidates at the last minute without a plan or checkerboard in place. They're immediately limited by what will be in stock because there's not enough time to replenish the right item before the ad hits the street. These limitations then create a domino effect, which can lead the merchant to stray from the strategy and produce less-effective advertising. A simple example: the right ad offering might be to show a good-better-best lineup, but without stock or time to replenish the "better" item, you may impair the appeal of the offering. Lastly, proper ad planning can provide a direct tie to meeting the sales plan. It can serve as a guide or tool to ensure that you're on track against budget.

Basic Data and Information

Know Your Role   Product categories typically serve a specific, defined role in the overall assortment of a retailer. As an example, in grocery or drug stores, Coca-Cola at 79¢/2 liter, milk by the gallon, diapers and other products are considered traffic drivers. Some companies will formally assign "role" designations as a part of their business-planning process. When building an advertising plan for any product category, it begins by knowing the category role. Best Buy, for instance, labels each category of product as being in one of five roles: primary business driver (television), profit generator (MSN service, phones), traffic (music), convenience (batteries or film), or emerging (satellite radio).

Events   Identify the events and dates of the events that need to be planned for. A mail-order company may send out a monthly circular, statement stuffers, a 1:1 email, etc. Retailers may use ROP (Run of Press, a newspaper ad) or weekly circulars. These pieces become the foundation of your plan.

Sales Budget   Know your budget for sales and gross margin. A good plan will be mindful of the big picture, not just a specific event. Also, the buyer should be mindful of results and leave a record for the following year. For example, if 40% of a category's sales were done on ad the week before Memorial Day, that fact becomes a data point for the following year.

History   Minimally, a merchant should retain a rolling one year of advertising records and results. Planning for March begins with a look at last March. Was it your anniversary sale? Did your category have the front cover of the circular (much more valuable space than page 6)? Were there notes from the prior events, such as "Sold 5,000 sets of Christmas lights, but ran out day 1 of the seven-day ad"? This becomes an indicator for you—buy more!

The subtle result of poor planning is lost sales. Without good record keeping, forecasting, and planning, you may never realize the full potential of your ad.

Competition   Know what your competition is doing and what they've done in the past. Again, I recommend that a full year of files be kept for printed materials (circulars, newspaper clippings, direct mail). Electronic advertising can be captured as notes on the buyer's checkerboard or a manager's review document. Is April your biggest competitor's anniversary? Do they run a yearly sidewalk sale or big promotion each year? Does that mass merchant always begin back-to-school ads in August? Perhaps you'll start in July in order to grab mindshare early.

Ad Planning Tools

The   An ad production schedule is a tool that identifies
Production   the many events or efforts over time and identifies
Schedule   the steps taken to ensure that all parties meet the deadlines necessary to produce the ad. The sophistication and degree of detail in a production schedule will vary based on need and the business.

Call Letter   Initiates an effort. Simply a formal way of letting people know that there will be an insert on May 4, an ROP on May 8, and so forth. Larger retailers may publish a more formal guide to detail the events of a month or a quarter.

*Sales
Candidates
Due*

Each buyer submits his ad candidates. This indicates a bid process, which is often used. It can create a healthy competition amongst the merchants to get the best ad items. Some environments simply allocate the space, and the "candidate submission" process is not really a competition.

*Final Item
Selection*

Decisions are made that enable the buyer to solidify a vendor deal, place orders for goods to support the ad, order photo samples, and generally move forward.

*Item Specs in
the System*

Loading all SKU-level detail or passing the information on to advertising so that creative work can begin.

First Proof

Buyers review the layout and creative work. Provide input and scrutinize details. (Logo usage: Does the item match the photo? Is copy accurate on features and benefits of the product? Are prices correct?)

Final Proof

Usually a minimum of two proofs is needed. This allows an opportunity to be sure that corrections made in the first proofing session were accomplished. Also, most retailers want one last shot or review of retail prices before an ad goes to print.

To Printer

The ad is out the door and can no longer be modified. Occasionally, a senior executive will want to call the printer or make a change because of a late competitive issue, but this should be rare.

Street Date

Ad appears in public.

The following is a basic example of what a production schedule might look like:

Event	May 4 Insert 24 page	May 8 Mothers' Day Full page ROP	May 11 Insert 12 page	May 18 Insert 24 page	May 22 Midweek 12 page tab Pre-Memorial Day	May 25 Insert 24 page
Call letter	2/11	3/11	2/18	2/25	2/25	3/4
Sale Candidates Due	3/11	4/8	3/18	3/25	3/25	4/1
Final Item Selection Made	3/18	4/15	3/25	4/1	4/1	4/8
Item Specs in System	3/25	4/17	4/1	4/8	4/8	4/15
First Proof	4/8	4/24	4/15	4/22	4/22	4/29
Final Proof	4/15	5/1	4/22	4/29	4/29	5/6
To Printer	4/18	5/5	4/25	5/2	5/2	5/9
Street Date	5/4	5/8	5/11	5/18	5/22	5/25

This is a simple example of a production schedule for the merchant group. Take it as illustrative. Depending on the needs of a particular company, this can be made much more elaborate by including many additional steps such as "photo samples due" or "request store signage." Also, this same type of tool may be used by other parts of the organization. An advertising department, for example, will often use a similar production schedule for their copywriters, layout artists, photo studio, and outside contractors.

The Checkerboard

The checkerboard is a basic tool of the merchant. It is a tool that helps the buyer to organize his promotional activity and plan the selection of items for ads. Its purpose is to provide a logical approach to planning, act as a sanity check to an assortment's planned advertising and provide efficiency.

Ideally, an ad plan and checkerboard should be constructed by quarters, three one-month periods, to allow for visibility and continuity. A lesser period of time can be limiting and may not provide enough event visibility to prevent promotion overlap. Many merchants will plan more than a quarter. I'm an advocate of advanced planning, but I also realized that the further forward you go, the possibility of change and ad revisions will increase.

The concept is simple. Think of a spreadsheet. Events are listed across the top. Products are listed down the side. Where each cell of intersection occurs, the merchant denotes that the item is or is not in the ad (as simple as placing an X in the squares). As an example:

Film Assortment	4/27 insert	5/4 insert	5/11 insert	5/18 insert	5/22 midweek	5/25 insert
Private Label 200 ASA, 24+3 exp. 4 pk	X			X	X	
PrivateLabel 400 ASA, 24+3 exp. 4 pk	X			X	X	
KodakStandard 100 ASA, 24 exp. 3 pk		X				X
Kodak Standard 200 ASA, 24 exp. 3 pk	X	X		X		X
Kodak Standard 400 ASA, 24 exp. 3 pk		X				X
Kodak Gold 100 ASA, 24 exp. Single			X			
Kodak Gold 200 ASA, 24 exp. Single			X			
Kodak Gold 400 ASA, 24 exp. Single			X			
Kodak Gold 100 ASA, 24 exp. 3 pk						
Kodak Gold 200 ASA, 24 exp. 3 pk	X		X			

KodakGold 400 ASA, 24 exp. 3 pk							
Private Label OTUC Camera 200 ASA 24+3 exp. 2 pk		X					X
Kodak OTUC Camera 200 ASA 24+3 exp. Single	X			X			
Kodak OTUC Camera 200 ASA 24+3 exp. w/flash Single	X			X			
Kodak OTUC Camera 200 ASA 24+3 exp. waterproof Single						X	
Polaroid Film 12 exp. 2 pk						X	

Notes

1. 5/4 and 5/25: $1 rebate in effect on Kodak
2. 5/22 midweek: Buy one get one free promo, save $5 on waterproof camera for Memorial Day

Extend the checkerboard out for a full three months and the rhythm emerges. A good-better-best (with private label as "good," Kodak as "better," and Kodak Gold as "best") week is followed by exposing the basic assortment in terms of speed (100, 200, 400 Kodak film). Week 3 moves to Gold, a higher price point and higher gross margin. A balance between private label and brand is seen each week. One-time-use cameras (OTUC) receive regular exposure for two probable reasons. First, they're a higher price point to put more dollars in the register. Second, the outdoor season is beginning (a popular time for this product). And May is a big month for weddings and graduations, a perfect time for OTUCs.

The checkerboard can be taken to great levels of sophistication depending on need, interface to other departments, and the purposes for which it's used. A buyer might dress it up by adding a column for retail price after the item descriptions. Cost and/or gross margin can be meaningful additions. In place of the "X," a buyer might place the actual retail for that event and gain a good visual of how prices line up.

When you think of higher ticket goods, like televisions or computers, this can be most helpful to ensure coverage within price bands. You might have an offering in the $199 range, the $299 range and the $399 price band. This appeals to different segments or to consumers who have a specific price range in mind or budget to spend. It offers a broader appeal than say $194, $199, and $188.

If inventory control or projection responsibility falls to the buyer, he might replace the "X" with a projection of unit sales. However that block or cell is used, it still indicates that a specific item is intended to be advertised in the correlating event.

The checkerboard used by a prominent national electronics retailer includes the SKU number of the product, a description, a model number (important in electronics), the vendor, cost, MAP (minimum advertised price—see "Pricing"), if applicable, and regular retail price. Each item in the left column has a line for unit, revenue, gross margin, and ASP (Average Sale Price) forecast. Certain rows tally up to provide a forecast of sales and gross margin for the ad.

Q1 Print Advertising
Promo Checkerboard - (Category)

SKU	Description	Model	Vendor	Cost	Retail		March 3rd Forecast	March 3rd Actual	March 10th Forecast	March 10th Actual
1234567	Product X	T	Sony	$144.65 MAP	$199.99 $189.99	Units	1000	893		
						Revenue	$189,990	$169,661		
						GM$'s	$45,340	$40,488		
						Ad Price / ASP	$189.99	$188.67		
						Points / Off Shelf Display	10	Yes		
1234567	Product X	T	Sony	$144.65 MAP	$199.99 $189.99	Units				
						Revenue				
						GM$'s				
						Points / Ad Price				
						Off Shelf Display				
1234567	Product X	T	Sony	$144.65 MAP	$199.99 $189.99	Units				
						Revenue				
						GM$'s				
						Points / Ad Price				
						Off Shelf Display				
1234567	Product X	T	Sony	$144.65 MAP	$199.99 $189.99	Units	1000	893		
						Revenue	$189,990	$169,661		
						GM$'s	$45,340	$40,488		
						Points / Ad Price	$10.00	$188.99		
						Off Shelf Display				
1234567	Product X	T	Sony	$144.65 MAP	$199.99 $189.99	Units	1000	893		
						Revenue	$189,990	$169,661		
						GM$'s	$45,340	$40,488		
						Points / Ad Price	$10.00	$188.99		
						Off Shelf Display				
1234567	Product X	T	Sony	$144.65 MAP	$199.99 $189.99	Units	1000	893		
						Revenue	$189,990	$169,661		
						GM$'s	$45,340	$40,488		
						Points / Ad Price	$10.00	$188.99		
						Off Shelf Display				

Print Ad Totals		March 3rd Forecast	March 3rd Actual	March 10th Forecast	March 10th Actual
	Units	4000	3572		
	Revenue	$759,960	$678,644		
	GM$'s	$181,360	$161,952		
	Points / ASP	$219.99	$189.66		
	Print Ad Promo Goal				

As a manager of merchants, I reviewed promotional checkerboards every quarter. The review was about fundamentals.

- [ ] Is there a plan?
- [ ] Does the plan support our strategy?
- [ ] Does the plan support key events (All on Sale, BOGO, One-cent Sale) of the company?
- [ ] Are items spread responsibly? I don't want to see the same item on sale four weeks in a row.
- [ ] Is there balance within price bands?
- [ ] Is forecast accuracy an issue?
- [ ] Does the ad projection fit into our financial goals/plans?

Manager's Tool

As a merchandise manager, it is always important to know that a sensible, balanced promotional plan is in place for each category of merchandise. Also, I always like to know that the plan will deliver on our financial objectives. The manager's tool can easily be adapted to any business. It is meant to provide a one-page snapshot of the month's promotional activity at a high level. It does not provide SKU-level detail (that's the checkerboard

Class	LY 32 page cat. 08/12/2002	TY 24 page cat. 08/01/2003	LY 24 page cat. 08/09/2002	TY 32 page cat. 08/08/2003	LY 32 page cat. 08/16/2002	TY 32 page cat. 08/15/2003	LY 24 page cat. 08/23/2002	TY 24 page cat. 08/22/2003	LY Total Space	TY Total Space
Personal Portables	40% 10% F.C.	40%	40% WTM/TY Promo	50%	50% 10% F.C. & Ultra ESP story	40% Sony event	40%	40% 10% B.C.	190% ++ F.C.	180%
Volume	$2,400,000.00	$2,865,000.00	$2,425,000.00	$2,890,000.00	$2,357,000.00	$2,818,000.00	$2,725,000.00	$3,268,000.00	$9,907,000.00	$11,841,000.00
Ad Volume	$534,620.00	$768,909.00	$486,080.00	$825,418.00	$834,846.00	$795,986.00	$1,059,849.00	$727,585.00	$2,978,456.00	$3,231,870.00
% Ad	22%	27%	20%	29%	35%	28%	39%	22%	30%	27%
Boom Boxes	20%	20%	20%	20%	20%	20%	20%	20%	80%	80%
Volume	$1,399,000.00	$1,270,000.00	$1,485,000.00	$1,350,000.00	$1,550,000.00	$1,410,000.00	$1,451,000.00	$1,329,000.00	$5,885,000.00	$5,359,000.00
Ad Volume	$282,000.00	$228,000.00	$337,000.00	$254,000.00	$471,000.00	$321,000.00	$491,000.00	$300,000.00	$1,581,000.00	$1,103,000.00
% Ad	20%	18%	23%	19%	30%	23%	34%	23%	27%	21%
Shelf Systems	30%	30%	20% 10% F.C.	40% 10% B.C.	50%	30% 10% B.C.	20%	30% 10% B.C.	130%	160%
Volume	$2,628,000.00	$3,047,000.00	$2,743,000.00	$3,164,000.00	$2,800,000.00	$3,242,000.00	$3,080,000.00	$3,567,000.00	$11,251,000.00	$13,020,000.00
Ad Volume	$373,000.00	$658,000.00	$567,000.00	$863,000.00	$510,000.00	$994,000.00	$425,000.00	$1,095,150.00	$1,875,000.00	$3,610,150.00
% Ad	14%	22%	21%	27%	18%	31%	14%	31%	17%	28%
Car-Fi	90%	90%	90%	90% 10% F.C.	90% 10% F.C.	90% 20% B.C.	80%	90%	360%	380%
Volume	$4,233,000.00	$5,885,000.00	$3,751,000.00	$5,218,000.00	$3,700,000.00	$5,150,000.00	$3,870,000.00	$5,385,000.00	$15,540,000.00	$21,638,000.00
Ad Volume	$631,596.00	$2,146,438.00	$936,650.00	$868,265.00	$927,695.00	$1,851,067.00	$479,480.00	$1,379,632.00	$2,975,421.00	$6,245,402.00
% Ad	15%	36%	25%	17%	25%	36%	12%	26%	19%	29%
Total Space	180	180	170	200	210	180	160	180	760	800
Total Volume	$10,660,000.00	$13,067,000.00	$10,404,000.00	$12,622,000.00	$10,407,000.00	$12,620,000.00	$11,126,000.00	$13,549,000.00	$42,583,000.00	$51,858,000.00
Commons			Shelf - Free sub Car - Free install promo		Car - Free speakers					

Notes: Competition ran a big sale in week two.

Manager's Tool

Take a few moments to familiarize yourself with the document. For this illustration, I have used audio as an example. The key classes or departments within that division are personal portables, boom boxes, shelf systems, and car audio. The principles should apply to most businesses. Take the following as an example:

Office Furniture

- Desk/Case goods
- Chairs
- Filing
- Folding tables
- RTA/Work centers
- Chair mats

Holiday Christmas

- Trim-a-Tree
- Outdoor lighting
- Decoratives
- Greeting cards
- Wrapping paper
- Gift items

Health and Beauty Care (HBC)

- Shampoo/Conditioner
- Toothpaste
- Mouthwash
- Analgesics
- Foot care
- Eye care

The components of the monthly ad overview are as follows:

1. Class or product grouping identification (personal portables, keyboards, etc.).

2.   Events (thirty-two-page catalog, twenty-four-page catalog, direct mail). Events are noted at the top of the form with drop dates (the date the ad takes effect). Seeing this information at a glance can alert me to any significant gaps. For example, there was a midweek last year that we don't have this year. Or a twenty-four-page book has been expanded to thirty-two pages.

3.   Comp Space. This year versus last year (TY vs. LY). When the template is created, actual space is recorded for the prior year, and the projected or planned space for future months is placed in the "TY" column. Once the ad date is past, the space for TY should be verified. It then populates the template for the same month next year.

The comparison is important to see at a glance how space compares from one year to the next. One full page last year compared to one-half page this year will be a problem if you expect to comp last year's sales for the week. As a manager, I may decide to fight for more space now, well before it's too late to adjust or risk my sales plan.

This particular tool also calls out key space such as front cover (FC) or back cover (BC). Cover space tends to be much more visible and valuable and will, therefore, impact projections and a sales plan.

4.   Volume/Ad Volume. This is the sales volume of the category for both TY (obviously a projected number) and LY (actual results). This year's number should be the most current forecast for the category. In some cases, this may be the budget.

Ad dollars are the projected sales for items to be advertised (may be taken from the checkerboard) for this year and actual ad item sales from the prior year.

5.   % Ad. This is simply calculated from the prior numbers. It serves as an indicator or barometer for the manager. If 25% of a category's business was generated from advertised merchandise using fifty points (half a page) of space last year yet only 10% is coming from the same space this year, some

probing is called for. Are there stock issues? Is the buyer picking powerful items? Are there fewer items being shown in the same amount of space?

Again, the form is a tool to keep you on track and meet the plan.

6. Bottom Totals. A summary of the space and dollars for a particular week or event. In the lower right-hand corner, the totals provide a quick look at the month. As a manager, you'll want to compare the volume TY vs. LY and the space TY vs. LY for a sanity check. Also, if the ad volume is 10% of your monthly budget, but historically you run 30%, reason suggests that the plan is not sound. It needs rework.

7. Comments. This space is used for key notations that will be helpful in understanding the plan or the year-over-year comparisons. A special buy that cannot be replicated may have caused ad volume (as a percent to total) to soar. Significant promotions, competition insights (Chain XYZ Anniversary Sale), and other noteworthy events can be captured here.

8. This manager's tool is fairly easy to maintain once it's initially set up. The LY column is filled in with critical space or sales. After a month end, the following year's template can be created with the LY columns filled in. The TY columns are filled with plan information and forecasted dollars. Again, when the event date passes, TY needs to be updated (forecast replaced by actual sales, percent of ad volume estimate by actual, etc.) in order to set up the next calendar year.

Odds and Ends

Strategy or Philosophy An ad plan should align with and support the company philosophy or strategy. For example, if the retailer is an EDLP (Every day Low Price) format, the buyer would not be cutting price on ad items. Such actions would confuse the customer and damage the brand.

Historical Data	Don't underestimate the importance of history. Collect competitive ads. Make notes on TV or radio events. National Hardware month for Sears was October last year. It's a safe bet that they'll declare October of next year "Hardware Month." And October of the next year, and so on.
	Recognizing these patterns can help in your planning or possibly give you an advantage. I wonder if Home Depot or Lowes is considering making September their National Hardware Month. Can Retailer XYZ gain an advantage by breaking their back-to-school ads a week earlier than Chain ABC? Retail chains need to improve comp sales of the prior year every month. These are lessons in history.
Good Items Will Sell	Drive the winners is a basic rule of thumb for retail. When an item or promotion works, don't be afraid to repeat it or work it into your ad rhythm.
Post Mortems	From the Latin "after death." On key events, it's usually worth the time to look back at the results and review what worked versus what didn't work (do a post mortem). This can provide tremendous insight for the following year.

Free delivery or free installation or all-on-sale events are often repeated with a regular rhythm because they work. So while a category cannot be "all-on-sale" every week (or by law, the sale price becomes your regular price), a merchant may run it quarterly or monthly, and it will always drive business.

In the end, there is no substitute for diligent ad planning to achieve success. Too often, I have seen buyers scramble to turn ad items in to their advertising group. Without pre-planning, there is little or no opportunity to gain vendor support. That's lost money. The probability of inventory problems will rise. That's customer disappointment. The lost efficiency and lost dollars to your bottom line that result from poor planning can never be recouped.

Chapter Eight

INVENTORY BASICS

E very merchant needs a basic understanding of inventory control and replenishment in order to be effective in the buying function. Why? A retail merchant is responsible for a category or categories of merchandise. The merchant will source product (pick the vendor), negotiate cost and program, set retail pricing, determine the advertising of the products, and deal with returns or end of lifecycle issues. Basically, he owns the merchandise from cradle to grave, and the inventory aspects of this ownership are undoubtedly one of the most important factors in making a profit.

This "cradle to grave" mentality became very clear to me early in my career as a merchant. I was working at Quill Corporation, the nation's largest mail-order supplier of office products, and just beginning to learn the merchant role. One day, I was receiving instruction from Dave Zamost, our buyer of furniture and electronics, when his phone rang. It was the warehouse manager calling. Apparently, a truck driver had shown up at the docks intoxicated. Our warehouse people wanted some direction on what to do so they called . . . the buyer. At the time, Dave told me, "Get used to it. In this chair, you own everything that's associated with your product categories." He was right.

Roll the clock forward twenty years. I'm working for a $20-billion retailer that employs three-hundred-plus inventory people. The president of the company is touring stores, sees open shelves in several areas, and calls . . . you guessed it . . . the buyer. It simply goes with the turf. So realize that the merchants are ultimately responsible.

That's why basic inventory knowledge is important to the successful buyer.

Today, most large organizations have a separate inventory department. It sets up the yins and yangs of buying. Merchants are passionate. Buyers love products, and when a product is selected for the assortment, they certainly believe it will sell, sell, sell! The role of inventory is to balance this enthusiasm and take a less-passionate view of the items. They purchase goods in reasonable increments that will effectively use the company's money while maintaining a high level of service. While selection and replenishment can be done by one person, it is almost an unnatural act that will almost always lead to overstock and transition problems.

Replenishment

Basic replenishment theory is actually fairly simple. There are five pieces to the puzzle. They are as follows:

1. History—Sales history in a consistent increment (weekly) is an essential building block. Most items are remarkably consistent in their sales performance. Downward trends are usually identifiable and can be projected. New items surges can be planned for or patterned off of like items.

   Many years ago, I worked for a small regional office-products chain in South Florida. Our flagship store was in North Miami Beach. Every month, that store sold 125 HON four-drawer vertical files. It always amazed me, but month after month, 125 file cabinets went out the door. So after twenty years, one would think that every man, woman, and child would have a four-drawer file. After all, they don't wear out, and they seldom break. Still, every month, 125 were sold. It was really a testament to predictability.

2. Lead time—This is typically the amount of time from when a purchase order is placed (phoned, faxed, transmitted) until the order leaves the vendor's dock. Some companies define

lead time as the amount of time from when a purchase order is received until the goods actually arrive at their store or warehouse. It's important to clearly define this period of time so that you and the supplier are in sync. It's not from order placement to order entry. It's not from order placement to invoicing. Miscommunication on lead time can result in stock outs.

3. Frequency of Review—How often is a supplier reviewed for ordering purposes? DSD products (Direct Store Delivery, such as milk, bread, snacks) are usually ordered daily. More conventional goods may be reviewed weekly, monthly, and even quarterly. Some products (like seasonal) are even reviewed annually.

    A number of factors come in to play when determining frequency. Let's suppose the vendor's minimum order for prepaid freight is $5,000. If you sell $200 of product each day, there is no point in reviewing the line daily or even weekly. Monthly may be your best option.

4. Shipping or Transit Time—Is the supplier down the street or across the nation? Will goods ship in full truckloads, LTL (Less than Trailer Load), or UPS? Each method has a different shipping time. If the goods are imported, this piece is particularly important.

5. Safety Stock—How much additional stock is required to protect you in the event of a lost order, a sudden surge in sales, a flat tire, or any other adverse impact to the supply chain?

    Safety stock is not meant to be a 100% insurance policy. Too much will slow turn. It's simply meant to be a hedge against breaks in predictability. Bread, milk, and other perishables are examples of products that should have little or no safety stock. A retailer might carry two or three weeks of safety stock on batteries, as it's more important to be in stock than it is to stretch your turn. Yet no amount of safety stock on batteries will cover a store in the event of a hurricane.

Systems, both manual and computerized, will use these five factors as a basis for replenishment. A simplistic method may define factors 2-4 in terms of weeks and add the number of weeks together to achieve a multiplier. A look backwards at sales (prior inventory plus open orders less current inventory equals sales) for several like periods can provide an average sales number. That's the history part or the fifth piece. That number times your multiplier will provide need. Need less on-hand inventory should equal the quantity to order. Confused? Let's try an example:

Lead Time	=	2 weeks
Shipping Time	=	2 weeks
Order Frequency	=	Every 2 weeks
Safety Stock	=	2 weeks

Added together, your multiplier is 8.

Assume that over the past four two-week periods of time, you have sold 150 units, 250 units, 225 units, and 175 units. Added together divided by 4, and the average period sales are 200 units (your history).

200 (average sales) X 8 (multiplier) = 1600 (need)
1600—on hand (let's say 1000)—any open orders (let's say 400) = quantity to order. In this example, it is 200.

It's simplistic, but it's foundational. Methods and systems will add complexity to this base as needed to constantly improve on the key goals of being in stock yet turning the inventory. For example, a promotional retailer may add promo forecasts into the equation. Promotional activity will impact the predictability of sales.

Communication

Good inventory control begins with good communication. Specifically, the buyer must provide the details of his plan to the inventory group for purchasing. These details include the source of products (vendor data) and the specifics around each item to be purchased (item data). Typically, retailers have specific forms in place to facilitate this communication. One such basic form is the Vendor Data Form. While elements may vary from one retailer to the next, there are basics that every merchant needs to capture.

A. Name and Address—Be specific. A corporate address may differ from a purchase order address or a remittance address or a sales contact address. All are important. Although most companies now use EDI (Electronic Data Interface) for placing, tracking, and receiving orders, it's still a good practice to capture the proper addresses.

B. Payment Terms—Often a key factor in the timing of order placement.

C. Lead Time—A key element of replenishment.

D. Minimum Order—Orders for less than minimum may be rejected or sold at a higher cost. Typically, this is the lowest dollar amount or quantity that a vendor will accept as an order. In some cases, there may be a different minimum in order to qualify for prepaid freight (Minimum order: $100; Prepaid Freight: $5,000).

E. Freight—The terms for shipping the goods (more to follow).

F. Returns Policy—Direction on how to deal with returned merchandise. Common policies include RTV (Return to Vendor), destroy in field (usually an allowance will offset any cost), return for repair or replacement. If returned goods are to be sent back to the vendor, be sure to clarify the freight terms.

G. Allowances—The Vendor Data Form is a place to recap allowances. As a communication vehicle, the form may be the means of advising the inventory group or accounts payable group about requirements to achieve the allowances. Throughout the years, I have created numerous vendor data forms. The following is typical:

See the next page for an example of a Vendor Data Form.

VENDOR DATA SHEET

VENDOR

NAME	NUMBER
ADDRESS	
CITY	STATE	ZIP
PHONE	( )

DATE: _____ BY: _____

LEAD TIME: _____
MINIMUM ORDER: _____
VENDOR UPC NUMBER: _____

ORDER ADDRESS (if different)

NAME	
ADDRESS	
CITY	STATE	ZIP
CONTACT	PHONE: ( )

FREIGHT TERMS

☐	PREPAID	MIN: _____
☐	PREPAY AND ADD	
☐	COLLECT	
☐	OTHER	

F.O.B. POINT: ☐ Destination
☐ Shipping Point

COMMENTS: _____

SALES INFORMATION

SALESPERSON	
REP FIRM	
ADDRESS	
CITY	STATE	ZIP
PHONE	( )

REMITTANCE INFORMATION

NAME	
ADDRESS	
CITY	STATE	ZIP
ACCOUNT CONTACT	
PHONE	( )

STANDARD PAYMENT TERMS:

ALLOWANCES

DISPLAY	:
VOLUME	:
NEW STORE:	:
PROMOTIONA	:
CO-OP	:
DETAILS	:

NOTI Programs should be confirmed in writing.

COSTS AND MARGINS BASED ON:

RETURN POLICY

☐	Return for Credit RETURN FREIGHT
☐	Return for Replacement	☐ Prepaid
☐	Other	☐ Prepay & Add

Authorization: ☐ Needed
☐ Not Needed

PRODUCT LIABILITY COVERAGE

Company requires that any new source provide a Certificate of Product Liability Insurance Coverage naming the Company as an additional insured.

COMMENTS/NOTES:

BUYER'S CHECKLIST

☐ Manufacturer's Catalog	☐ Flammable Materials	☐ Warranty Information
☐ Samples	☐ Guaranteed Sale on Tests	☐ Shelf Life Considerations
☐ Price List	☐ 6-month Price Protection	☐ Pre-pricing
☐ Internet Content	☐ Private Label Potential	☐ Floor Stocking
☐ Display	☐ Feature/Benefit Discussion	Possibilities

As a final note on vendor data, larger retailers will often drive a more comprehensive vendor agreement. It becomes a legal document and can be very broad in nature. The vendor information in the above form is really meant to be universal in nature. Contract or not, the merchant needs this basic information.

A second key communication tool is the Item Specification Form. This will provide the item-level detail needed by multiple departments to perform their tasks. For example, if a product has a case pack of twenty-four, the rebuyer would not order in increments of fifteen.

Generally, this document serves as a data entry form to load products specs into a system. Various departments (inventory, warehousing, accounting) may have access to the information as needed to do their job. Many retailers now offer Internet capabilities and have their vendors submit all new items by providing all of the required information. A typical form may cover the following:

A. Classification—By assigning a department, class, subclass, or group identification to an item, it can be aggregated with like items to roll up sales information. For example, I may want to know last week's revenue for soup as a category rather than every SKU of soup.

B. UPC Number—Used for scanning merchandise.

C. Description—A description should explain the product in a detailed fashion. A business may specify the number of characters available in their corporate system for descriptions. I've seen forms ask for a second mini-description that will print on the cash register tape or the shelf tag in a store.

D. Cost Detail—The unit of measure. Do you order in "each," "boxes," "dozens," or "cases"? These and other cost details enable the rebuyer to land goods in the most effective manner.

E. Projection of Sales—The buyer needs to provide some estimates of sales as a guide until history is accumulated.

The following Item Specification Form on the next page is a basic example, although required data may vary greatly from retailer to retailer based on industry and system.

Page ___
of ___

NEW ITEM SPECIFICATION SHEET

VENDOR _____

VENDOR NO. _____

PRODUCT DEPT/CLASS _____

Page: _____   Price Label Code _____

DATE _____

☐ Add to Catalog
☐ Shelf Life Considerations
☐ Warranty Info to File
☐ Private Label
☐ Non-Taxable

FREIGHT

☐ Prepaid Min. _____
☐ Prepay & Add _____
☐ Collect (If applicable at item level) _____

BUYER'S COMMENTS:

	PRODUCT DETAIL					COST DETAIL						SELLING DETAIL			
MFG STOCK NO. UPC NO.	DESCRIPTION (25 characters)	COLOR CODE	CTN QTY CTN WT	MIN STORE ORDER QTY	MFG LIST	U/M	NET COST	INBOUND FREIGHT	EXTRAS	SELL COST	RETAIL	PER U/M	G.P. %	EST. MONTHLY USAGE PER STORE
1														
2														
3														
4														
5														
6														
7														
8														
9														

Freight, Shipping, Transportation

These terms refer to the movement of goods from the supplier to the retailer. How is the merchandise delivered? Who pays for the expense? Who owns the merchandise while in transit? These questions are answered by determining the freight program for each vendor.

Essentially, there are three options here (prepaid, prepay and add, and collect) and the buyer should be familiar with each, as freight is a key factor in the landed cost of goods. Here's what you need to know:

PREPAID: When goods are shipped prepaid, the cost of transportation is included or buried in the net cost. There is no additional charge for freight.

Advantages
- The vendor assumes the responsibility for shipment.
- The vendor arranges the carrier.
- There is no additional invoice for freight (less hassle).
- The vendor can often move goods much faster and for less than the retailer.
- Freight increases in the industry do not affect the sell cost as easily.

Disadvantages
- The true cost of an item may be hidden by the freight.
- The retailer cannot specify which carrier to use (although many vendors will comply with their wishes if possible).
- Carrier discounts may or may not be passed on. That is, the supplier may negotiate a better rate and keep it inside.

PREPAY AND ADD: Under such terms, a vendor will pay transportation costs and simply add charges to the invoice.

Advantages
- The retailer sees freight bills.
- Computer costs are "cleaner." The retailer has a cost for the product, plus freight, which equals the sell cost or laid-in cost.

Disadvantages
- This can be extra work for traffic, A/P, and pricing functions.
- Industry increases in freight, ordering patterns, or growth will alter the "factor" that is built in. The retailer has no

good means of control. For example, a company that I worked for once stocked a cash register, which was shipped from California. The buyer estimated sales to be fifty units per month and added a $2 per unit freight factor. Many months later, we realized that sales were not as expected and inventory control was purchasing one or two machines at a time. They were buying weekly quantities rather than monthly. The freight for one machine from California was about $18. As a result, we were under priced, and the item was unprofitable.

- Discounts can be hidden.

COLLECT: Under such terms, the source assumes no responsibility for the transportation of merchandise. The carrier will bill the store or retailer for freight costs.

Advantages
- The retailer controls the movement of goods.
- The retailer can choose the carrier.
- The retailer will see and pay for the freight bills.
- The retailer has more control over the freight factor.

Disadvantages
- It is additional work for traffic, A/P, and pricing functions.
- Sell costs are subject to error as a result of changes in the freight factor. For example, suppose that you buy paper and have 5¢ per ream added for freight. A ream of paper has a cost of say $2, plus 5¢ for freight. Therefore, your landed or "sell" cost is $2.05 per ream. Buyers will calculate gross margin from the landed cost. Now, if freight costs increase and become 7¢ per ream, there is a risk of gross-margin erosion if the buyer doesn't know and make an adjustment.

FOB POINT—The FOB Point is the point at which ownership of the merchandise changes hands. FOB factory means that the retailer assumes ownership at that point. FOB retailer or destination means that the vendor owns the merchandise until it's delivered. The acronym stands for freight on board.

Notes on Freight:

1   Freight is a critical-cost component which needs to be monitored by the merchant. I have always advocated that freight be reviewed with any line review or when cost adjustments are made by the vendor.

2.   Freight in (from supplier to retailer) is only a part of the picture. Freight out must be considered in many circumstances. Does the retailer deliver? Mail order or Internet providers incur outbound freight expenses. Larger retailers will use distribution facilities. Costs of moving goods from the distribution center to stores becomes a factor.

3.   Larger retail organizations usually prefer "Collect" terms. They have capabilities of moving the freight, and they gain a sense of true cost of goods by not mixing freight cost and product cost as in a "Prepaid" situation.

Odds and Ends

In-stock Position—A key element of the retail game is being in stock on an item when the customer is ready to buy. Merchant interaction with the inventory group is critical to good balance. When considering dropping items or replacing a line, these teams must work closely and communicate regularly to ensure a smooth transition. In a perfect world, the last piece of the old item is sold when the first shipment of the new goods lands in a store.

Companies will measure their in-stock position in many ways. Is there one in stock, two in stock, a day's worth of sales, or some other quantity available for sale? Regardless of the measure, the idea is to never disappoint a customer.

Inventory Feedback—The merchant must be receptive to, indeed, seek out feedback from his inventory partner. The actual placing of orders and care for inventory will often unearth great opportunities for efficiency. An inventory analyst recently asked me if we might adjust the case pack to twelve rather than twenty-four and facilitate improved store replenishment on a product. The shelf holds twenty-four. Sending twenty-four leaves a back stock.

Bad Inventory—Nonsalable inventory is bad inventory. Products become discontinued. Customers return merchandise. Some products expire (toners, milk, batteries, foods) due to shelf-life limitations. Nonsalable inventory needs to be removed in order to keep open-to-buy dollars free for replenishment.

This can be quite difficult. Markdowns or write offs can destroy the P and L. Leaving bad merchandise unaddressed, however, is worse. It inhibits purchasing power, clogs shelves, and will do more to hurt your sales numbers than the write off to get rid of it. Mark it down, write it off, give it to charity, just get rid of it.

Price Changes—Merchants must always communicate cost or program adjustments in a timely manner. As a rule, I always required a minimum of sixty days advance notice of any cost change from a vendor. Retailers that produce catalogs or other printer material may seek longer time periods. Failure to advise the inventory group will certainly result in creating purchase orders at the wrong cost. Billing won't match the order. Invoices will be held up or not paid or not paid accurately. Eventually, this will come back to roost with the buyers.

GMROI—This term stands for gross margin return on investment. It's a key metric in measuring the effective use of money tied up in inventory. Although there is a formula for calculating this metric in its basic form, it's EARN times TURN. That is gross margin percent times inventory turn.

Owned Inventory—Another popular metric. This one essentially factors payment terms into the mix to determine how much of the inventory is actually owned by the retailer. An example of this in a practical sense is covered in the section on Payment Terms.

Floor Stocking—In an effort to facilitate improved customer service and keep inventory turning, some retailers will push vendors into a floor-stocking program. Here, a manufacturer will build extra product and hold it, ready to ship, until needed by the retailer. This can be a win for both parties.

I once employed this practice with several manufacturers of private-label envelopes. My commitment to the goods allowed them to create an efficient run and build a three-month supply of goods. It saved them money. I had the benefit of smaller minimum orders, shortened lead time, and reduced safety stock (they had plenty of safety). It was a win-win situation.

In the end, the merchant plays a vital role in the inventory-control portion of the business. So much so, in fact, that I will always advocate that any good merchant needs a tour of duty in the inventory chair. It will broaden one's perspective and give a look at merchandising from a different point of view.

Chapter Nine

THE "CLICK 'N' MORTAR" MERCHANT

In the late '90s, the retail world had to come to terms with the emergence of Internet commerce. Almost overnight, the safe haven or, at least, known haven of a physical environment came under attack from a virtual world where standard marketing, pricing, and profitability didn't seem to matter.

This new channel for commerce took off like a rocket and caught many retailers by surprise. Of course, the federal government was a powerful advocate for Internet development (Didn't Al Gore invent the Internet?). Also, e-tailers were exempt from collecting sales tax outside of their home state. This gave them a price advantage over retail. Yet perhaps the greatest catalyst for the development of Internet business was the investment community. Investment capital poured into this industry by the billions without holding start-ups accountable for results. Stock multiples and company valuations soared for e-tailers while good old brick-'n'-mortar companies were still held to traditional measures like quarterly earnings and profitability.

During this chaotic, fast-paced time, I was afforded the opportunity of serving as the vice president of merchandising for BestBuy.com. As the Best Buy Internet initiative began to get traction, it was quickly obvious that the merchant role would be a critical part of its development and the ongoing business activity. To a large degree, we pioneered "click 'n' mortar." At that time, there were no good models that might provide guidance on how a dot-com initiative might tap the merchant resource and work within a traditional retail company.

Clearly, retail organizations have two paths to choose from in terms of Internet development and support of ongoing operations. First, use their current merchant team. Simply leverage the current expertise to sustain a website. The alternative is to develop an Internet merchant team, which can be fully focused on dot-com yet leverage the strengths already present within the organization (vendor relationships, assortment planning, allowances). Until such time as e-commerce is literally in the DNA of a retail organization, I would advocate the latter path. Here's why:

1. *Devotion to the Medium and the Business of the Internet.*

     Developing or integrating any new business from within an organization is extremely difficult. Retail history is littered with examples of failure. Ben Franklin stores, for example, once tried to open an office-products superstore and failed miserably. It was 1986, and variety stores as a concept were well past their prime. The company knew that survival required new concepts, and they tried several. As a very small group tried to develop the Office-Station concept from within, they encountered roadblocks at every turn. The new concept needed real estate, but the Ben Franklin real estate group was busy. The new concept needed to leverage merchandising, but the merchants all had full time jobs and couldn't make the time. Ad support—same story. Store layout and design—same story. Even knowing that their future was at stake, the running of daily business was always the first priority. Today, Ben Franklin no longer exists.

     Ames Department Stores purchased Zayre in the late '80s. Has anyone seen a Zayre store lately? K-Mart developed and brought to market several new concepts. Office Square and Sports Authority are just two examples. Office Square was sold to Office Max, and Sports Authority was spun off as well. G.C. Murphy tried an office products superstore with Office Shoppe Warehouse. Tandy Corp. invented Incredible Universe. The list goes on and on.

A select few learn to operate different platforms within one company. Sears operated a robust catalog division and department stores for many years. Wal-Mart and their Sam's Club division are also good examples. Yet even these great retailers struggled with their Internet development. Note that these organizations developed independent merchant organizations to address different channels because they realized that the metrics, the operations, the very nature of the business was different even though they had one parent company. For example, Sam's Club has a buying staff focused on fast-turning products in well-defined limited categories. There are no fancy displays or fixtures. Wal-Mart merchants, however, are discount retail buyers. Each looks at product, pricing, packaging, and display needs very differently.

2. *Bench Strength*

The available headroom within a brick-'n'-mortar merchant group just isn't there. Most teams run at full speed every day to keep up with the business. Adding the Internet to their workloads would create overload, and on Friday, when there was a choice between proofing an ad for the core business, which pays the bills or working on the website . . . web loses every time.

3. *Building Merchant Expertise in a Virtual World*

The Internet is a new and different medium. Typically, retail merchants focus on shelf space, planograms, assortments, and inventory issues. Traditional retailers can find merchants with fourteen, twenty, even thirty years of experience. In a virtual world, the difference quickly becomes apparent.

- ☐ The need for deeper, richer copy.
- ☐ Photography requirements are vastly different.
- ☐ Selling tools move from shelf tags, training, and POP to shopping assistant, a glossary, search engines, FAQs, and comparison charts.

4.   *Promotional Planning*

The standard ad checkerboard and promotional tools become subpar when applied to the Internet. The net offers multiple levels of promotion, affiliate programs, personalization, and more. When I log on to Amazon.com the homepage says "Hello Daniel" and shows me several offerings on history books because they know that I'm an avid reader of history. When my neighbor logs on, the homepage says "Hello Michael" and shows him music and movies. Try to do that with a printed Sunday circular.

5.   *Measurements*

Key metrics are different between retail and e-tail. While both focus on sales and gross margin, the retail buyer is concerned about return on space, print ad effectiveness, etc. The e-tail buyer wants to measure hits, traffic, basket abandonment, order cancels, and such.

My experience has been that people that have not worked in an Internet environment will generally underestimate the workload of the dot-com merchant. The daily (often hourly) interface with publishing, the proofing activities, page-load issues, QA testing against various hardware and search engines, and virtual promotions all add up to a great deal of work. Adding that work to an existing retail-merchant group will either jeopardize the ongoing business or doom the website to mediocrity.

Strategy Needed

A click-'n'-mortar organization is the combination of traditional retail with an Internet presence. This special hybrid needs a clearly defined strategy in order to be effective and properly serve its customers. While it may look simple from afar, it is anything but simple. The dot-com division must compete in a virtual world against pure plays (Internet-only companies) that can move quickly. Click 'n' mortar, however, has two faces to the consumer, and each represents the brand. That's why a detailed strategy is imperative.

- Should consumers expect the same prices on line as they see in store, or vice versa? If so, what's the impact, and how do you execute? Most retailers have price zones (Chicago is different than Atlanta), but the website has one price.
- Can I buy online and return it to a store? Execution on such a promise is a systems' nightmare.
- If we only have one thousand pieces of a hot product (say a new movie release), who gets them? the web or the stores?
- Should promotions agree online and in store? It's easy to say yes, but it may not be practical. Free delivery is a great online promotion. Not so in store. Try to do a tent sale online or a product tasting.

Once the strategy is formulated, rules of engagement and team direction can be established. The following examples might be elements of "direction" or strategy. These were fundamental for BestBuy.com.

Assortments: As a general guideline, the online assortment will be a reflection of the SKUs (Stock Keeping Units) offered in store. The merchant may, however, deviate from the guideline when sound judgment and analysis provide a compelling reason to do so.

For example

1. SKU intensive product lines such as music, movies, software, and games can be more deeply assorted online than in store. It's a condition of physical space and inventory commitment.
2. In non-core categories the store may offer a good, better, best choice for consumers. Online, it may make sense to limit such an offering in order to save the expense of photography, copy, and publishing.
3. Packaging considerations. Film in a store is most often sold as a single unit, a three-pack, or some value-added package. When offered via the Internet, the buyer may opt to not assort the single packs. Multipacks are much more efficient for packing and shipping.

Expanded Assortments: Dot-com merchants may add SKUs beyond the standard (brick 'n' mortar) assortment where it is sensible to do so. The following guiding principles should apply.

1. Any product line extensions must align with the brick-'n'-mortar strategy. For example, the net merchant would not add a new vendor to the mix without prior discussion with their store counterpart.

2. All SKU additions must have an exit strategy (return to vendor, reduce prices with markdown dollars, etc.). The risk associated with adding these items should not be borne solely by the company. No exit strategy, no item.

3. Within each category, standard inventory turn goals and level of service must prevail. The additional SKUs should not degrade performance.

Pricing: The basic consumer experience should be one of synchronized every day prices between the stores and the Internet. Then, consider the channel differences. There will be occasions on which it makes sense to be at one price online while at another price in store, and consumers will accept it. Regional price reaction to competition, for example, cannot be executed on the Internet. Hourly specials or a "13-hour sale" can be difficult or impossible to execute online, but stores can easily handle them.

Additional rules or guidelines may be needed so that each channel can operate at maximum efficiency and not create confusion or conflict for the consumer or the vendors.

The point here is to communicate. Identify issues and resolve them. In most click-'n'-mortar situations, the stores are dominant and will be the primary caretakers of the vendor relationship (although that may change someday) except where the vendor is an Internet-only supplier. When conflict arises, such as which channel gets inventory on a limited product (the new Harry Potter book, the launch of a new gaming platform), resolve it and adjust or add to the "rules of engagement."

Merchant.Com Responsibilities

What are the specific responsibilities of the Internet merchant? Certainly, this will vary by company or industry, but the following top 10 may serve as a general outline:

1. **Represent the Internet channel on vendor selection and relationship.** Negotiate and maintain "programs," allowances, and co-op. Be the company's primary contact to the vendor for the following:

    *   Debit balances
    *   Post-audit claims
    *   Item-selection process
    *   Vendor-data maintenance
    *   Solicitation of ad participation
    *   Adherence to company agreements (MAP, logo usage)

2. **Product selection.** Defining the assortment (pricing, product data, specifications) and managing the assortment process. Resolving all product-related issues: samples, copy, and solutions. Define and manage the product-attribute definitions.

3. **Relationship with brick 'n' mortar.** Take a lead role in maintaining a strong relationship with the brick-'n'-mortar team. Neither side should "surprise" the other.

    Share information, programs, promotional plans, and other offers as needed. Resolve conflict/issues so as to best present a united single-mindedness to the vendors. Consider yourself a team member—vendor meetings, trade shows, critical projects—the two must be a sharing organization.

4. **Transition management.** Align with brick 'n' mortar as needed to ensure that product on the website is current and available. Assume responsibility for the communication of transition issues.

5. **Pricing.** Understand the competitive landscape, brick 'n' mortar, and vendor issues to keep the Internet business true to

the strategy. Achieve gross-margin goals. The buyer should be responsible for all maintenance to retails.

6. **Advertising.** Coordinate (if applicable) the promo activity of brick 'n' mortar with the net. Printed circulars and other events need to occur within Internet space as well. Maintain promo plans for net specific events.

7. **Visual merchandising.** Be a participant/leader in determining the visual presentation of products. The buyer will best know key features, good/better/best designations, complete solutions needs, vendor issues concerning presentation or logo usage, etc.

8. **Logical line extension.** The buying teams will extend lines of products as necessary. While retail may be optimizing an assortment due to shelf space or other issues, the E-tail group may carry more SKUs.

9. **Forecasting.** An important function. The Internet merchant needs to forecast appropriately and plan the business in order to purchase inventory, prepare for business surges (more people to answer phones), and so forth.

10. **Online store strategy.** The merchant will own the strategy online. How to buy guides, comparison charts, configurations, and other tools are to be employed as needed to enhance the consumer experience.

Content

The Internet is a content-rich medium, and most sites use content as a differentiator in the marketplace. Certainly, it sets a website apart from a retail store. Elements of content will vary by site and industry. For example, an airline site will usually offer vacation planning, frequent-flyer information, and powerful search engines for booking flights. Amazon will serve up editorial reviews, comments from others who bought a product or read a book, customer advice, multiple views, and more. The following are general elements of content that can be found on most e-tail sites.

Short Descriptions—A brief description of the product's features and benefits, often used in conjunction with a photo and price near the surface of a site. That is, when searching for a product (say a digital camera), a site may line them up with a short description in order to make the full assortment visible. A click on the picture will then open a single item to reveal greater content or a long description.

Photography—Every item on the website needs a picture. Complex items will often require multiple views, and the more advanced sites will offer the option to enlarge the pictures.

    Photo standards are an important issue within any site. For the sake of continuity, will the company shoot its own photo, accept vendor artwork, or grab art from other sites? Is it acceptable to show a product in its package, or does it need to be stand alone? Toys R Us, for instance, picture their action figures in action, not in the box.

Attributes—These are the specifics of a product. The shoes are size 10, medium width, and black in color. The legal pad is 8 ½ x 11, perforated top, 50 sheets, 12 per package, white paper. The camcorder weighs 4 pounds, has a 560X zoom, a lithium battery, and a 2.5-inch color screen. Attributes need to be well defined by product grouping. When done properly, consumers can easily line up like products to compare the attributes.

Product Reviews—A biased or unbiased (preferably the latter) synopsis of the product in use. Many websites purchase third-party content for reviews in the belief that "ZDNet" or "Consumer Reports" will add credibility to the site.

How-to-buy Guide—This provides assistance for the purchase of more sophisticated products. When

researching an automobile, for example, the consumer will
often find a guide, which prompts them with questions
designed to help them with a selection.

- Are you interested in a new or used auto?
- Does brand matter?
- Foreign or domestic?
- Color?
- SUV, van, or sedan?
- Two-door or four-door?

Glossary—a glossary is the place to define the terms or
unusual language of a product category. When shopping
for a camera, the glossary might have terms like APS, film
speed, zoom, LCD, and so forth, as a quick reference for
the reader.

Content can take many other forms (long description, helpful
articles on how to buy, frequently asked questions). The merchant
role in content will vary based on the company structure, but like
most things in retail, the buyer is most often responsible for it. The
merchant may need to procure content, write it, provide the details
for a copywriter to write it, or leverage the vendors for it. The buyer
will certainly proof it and be tasked to keep it fresh.

Additional Callouts for the Internet

Personalization. I shop at Amazon because they know me. Over time,
they have captured information about me, and from my browsing
and purchase history, they know what I like. When I last signed on,
they showed me several history books because I had just purchased
Of Gods and Generals by Shaara.

Pace. The speed of the Internet is incredible. Enacting a line change
or reset in a retail chain can take months. On the Internet, it can take
minutes. That's good and bad. A pricing error once cost my team

$60,000 in a day (the bad news). Once identified, we downloaded a fix within thirty minutes (the good news).

Search engines and BOTS crawl through sites for the best deals. Viral marketing is extraordinary. A hot product—word spreads fast!

Partner. The net is often about partnership. E-tailers partner in marketing (banner ads, pop up, affiliate programs), hosting, obtaining content, and much more. If one company has a good configurator, why reinvent it? Work a deal with them.

As a final note to retailers, manufacturers, sales reps, and other readers: cross pollinate. Send brick merchants to the Internet side and vice versa. As the intricacies and knowledge is shared, you'll build a stronger organization for the twenty-first century.

Chapter Ten

QUICK HITS

There are fundamental elements of merchandising that every buyer/merchant needs to know. I refer to these as the "blocking 'n' tackling" of buying. As the merchant role has morphed over time into more of a generalist, these basics have often been missed or, certainly, been less than fully understood. This work has taken a deep dive into several of the key elements associated with retail buying. There are, however, many more topics worthy of focus and review. Here are just a few:

Merchant Math

As my children were growing up, every time they whined about math ("Why do I have to learn this stuff?"), I answered that I apply math in my work every day. It's a basic need of the merchant.

There are volumes written on mathematics, even retail math. Many years ago, I would explain the basics to young buyers, such as the following:

> Price minus Cost = Gross Margin
> Gross Margin divided by Price = Gross Profit Percent

Eventually, I shortened the lesson to one sentence: buy a Texas Instrument BA-20 profit-manager calculator. This modern marvel is a basic calculator with memory and six extra keys for managing profit.

CST		SELL		MAR
SEL		CST		CST
MAR		MAR		SEL

Want to know cost? Enter the retail (SEL) and the margin (MAR) and the device calculates your cost.

Want to know the selling price? Enter cost (CST) and margin (MAR) and the device calculates retail or sell price.

Want to know gross margin? Enter cost (CST) and sell price (SEL) and the device calculates your gross margin.

The calculator is available in most office-products superstores in a solar-powered mini-desktop fashion. Sadly, Texas Instruments stopped making the pocket version years ago.

The Retail Floor

A good merchant is familiar with the operations of his store. Understanding the signage, shelf tags, shrink issues, returns process, labor issues, and policies of the store are invaluable reference points for the buyer. Many organizations advocate or require that merchants actually work in the stores on some regular basis (once monthly or quarterly) in order to see firsthand what occurs when product meets customer.

Seasonal

Seasonal buying is almost an art form unto itself. It requires a keen eye for what will sell, in combination with strong planning and organizational skills. Then add a heavy dose of grit and guts because seasonal merchandise can make you a hero or bum. I've seen a great seasonal plan on air conditioners and fans go completely BUST when the warm weather never showed up. What does one do with millions of dollars in snow blower and snow shovel inventory if it doesn't snow? Or if it snows too much, you're out of stock and disappointing customers.

In my experience, this category comes down to partners and plans. Find partners or vendors that have experience and will work closely with you to mitigate risk and leverage upside. As for planning, always look at a season in its entirety, maintain good records of sales for future planning, and do the math. For example, the following chart shows a seasonal plan for candles with a projection of gross margin after markdowns.

Halloween Candles

					Sell Thru 85%		Sell Thru 50% MD		Total Sales	
Item	Qty	Cost	Retail	GM	Retail	GM	Retail	GM	Retail	GM
Pumpkin Candle	13,176	4,900	10,145	51.0	8,623	51.0	747	1.8	9,384	49.66
Novelty	3,096	3,374	6,161	45.0	5,236	45.0	462	(9.0)	3,374	40.8
Ghost Candle	2,652	1,723	2,625	34.3	2,231	34.3	196	(31.0)	2,428	29.0
Gravestone	3,135	2,037	3,103	34.3	2,638	34.3	232	(31.0)	2,037	9.0
Tea Lights 10 Count	15,000	6,750	14,850	55.0	12,622	55.0	1,113	(9.0)	13,736	51.0
Votive Display	85	5,577	7,140	30.0	7,111	30.0	535	(40.0)	6,604	24.0
TOTAL		24,361	44,024	44.6	38,461	44.6	3,285	(11.0)	37,563	34.9

Here, the buyer assumes that 85% of the Halloween candles will sell thru at the original retail price. A 50% markdown will be taken on October 29 or 30 and the balance should sell thru quickly. If the plan works, there will be over $37,000 in sales at an all in gross margin of almost 35%. Like all seasonal plans, the buyer will need to monitor sales throughout the season. Strong sales will mean fewer goods sold as marked down. Or perhaps a 25% markdown will do the job. Conversely, weaker sales may adversely impact the plan.

The above spreadsheet is a single view of one modest category but is applicable to most seasonal products (lawn and garden, gift wrap, suntan lotion, etc.). As a merchandise manager for greeting cards, I once used a similar view for my Christmas season. The items were boxed cards, counter cards, ornaments, calendars, and gift wrap. Counter cards had no markdowns as a full returns program was in place. Boxed cards took a series of three markdowns—25% off ten days prior to Christmas, 50% off on December 26, and 75% off on

January 2. My goal, like the Halloween candle example, was a specific dollar volume at a specific gross margin.

I'll leave the subject of seasonal with two bits of advice:

1. Courage. If you have done the homework, reviewed the sales trends of prior years, and developed a sound plan, it still takes courage to stay the course. When the bosses are screaming for you to cut orders or take markdowns early, it will require nerve (and hopefully some facts) to remain on plan.

2. Your first markdown is the best markdown. Retail buyers that act timidly will usually be sitting with ice scrapers in July. Markdowns are not pleasant, but if needed, take it and take it deep.

Debit Balance

Most retailers periodically publish a debit balance (some call it credit balance) report. This is simply a list of vendors that owe you money. Although unusual, it does happen.

The creation of a debit balance is most often the result of a merchant not covering all the bases. A buyer discontinues doing business with a vendor and fails to advise accounting. Bills are paid, yet expense charges (possibly for returns or advertising or volume allowances) continue to build. Soon, there are no open invoices to deduct from and the supplier actually owes you money.

What to do?

1. Ask for it. Yes, many suppliers will want to keep the door open for future business and may pay any open debit.

2. Order something. If a vendor owes you money, placing an order may be your only option. While there may not be a fit for your assortment, better to take something than to leave an open issue.

3. Write it off. This may hurt, but if there is no hope of clearing up the debit, write it off.

4. Learn from it. What caused the debit balance? How can this
    be prevented in the future? If a new vendor replaced the
    old one, will they assume the debit? If the return policy is
    "return for credit," should it be changed prior to dropping
    the vendor?

Negotiating

Negotiating skills are a much-needed part of a merchant's tool
kit. Over the years, I have seen the spectrum from mediocre, unskilled
negotiators to some of the most masterful. Still, I have no silver bullet
for how to leave a negotiation feeling like a winner. What I can offer
is some perspective and context on the subject.

Dealing from a Position of Strength

Several years ago, I purchased an Audi A6. My negotiation with
the salesman was very simple. My twenty years of experience in
negotiating with some of the largest companies in America meant
nothing. The Audi was hot! The dealer sold every one he could get,
and there was a waiting list for the car. I wanted one. I paid full list,
just like everyone else. Surprisingly, however, I went away happy
believing that I had paid a fair price and been spared the agony of a
new car negotiation.

Retail is no different. Often, a buyer or a seller will find themselves
in a position of strength. It only makes sense to take advantage of
such a position, but remember to think about the big picture. My
Audi dealer sold the car at full list but gave me some upgraded mats,
offered free car washes, and explained the many services they offered.
He knew that my next purchase may come when there are plenty of
cars on the lot and wanted to be sure that I was treated fairly.

As the vice president of BestBuy.com during our start-up phase,
I was subjected to a painful experience in which I came up on the
short end. PDAs (Personal Digital Assistants) were a hot product and
Handspring was the hot vendor. When I first met with Handspring,
their executives laid out the wackiest, most insane program that I had

ever encountered from a vendor. Although Best Buy was already doing tens of millions of dollars in business with them through our retail stores, they insisted that we pay a higher cost per item for goods that were to be sold via the Internet. Their perverted logic was that it was more efficient and less expensive to sell via the Internet than it was to sell their product in a retail store. Therefore, they should make more money from the Internet channel. They insisted that we use separate purchase orders for goods to be sold on the net, even though the merchandise would be in the same warehouse location.

I invested countless hours trying to break through their flawed logic. After all, why would anyone believe that the net is less expensive than retail stores? At this time, no Internet sellers were making money. In the end, we simply didn't offer the product online. The story serves as a good example of having the power yet abusing it. Fast forward three years later—the PDA market was all but gone. You can bet we remembered the courteous treatment we received from Handspring.

Being Able to Say No

As a merchant, being able to say "no" is perhaps the best possible negotiating position to be in. I saw this firsthand during my experience at PharMor. PharMor, a deep-discount drug chain, was known for "Power Buying." The business was based on a formula of 162/3 markup and the company only bought deals. If the deal on Crest was 7.2 oz, they bought it. If the next week there was no deal on Crest, they simply wouldn't buy it. A week later, the deal might be a "25% more" package. Buy it. A two-pack—"buy one get one free"—buy it. Back to regular price—buy something else.

So, picture the grocery aisle. PharMor always had twelve to fifteen brands of cereal in stock but not necessarily the same brand every day. If you saw Rice Krispies, it was the best price in the marketplace. But stock up today because next week, Coco Puffs might be in that space.

What this did for the merchant was it empowered him to say no. There were no planograms that had to be maintained. If the

Quaker Oaks Company didn't serve up a phenomenal deal on their cereal, it wasn't purchased. We'd purchase General Mills. There was always a company that needed an order for thirty to forty truckloads of cereal.

Fact Based

Fact-based negotiation is a more structured approach. It removes much of the style and personality from the process and replaces it with logic and facts. In a fact-based approach, the buyer will sort through all relevant market and competitive data. He will develop a plan based on the role a category plays in the overall assortment. Before any vendor negotiation begins, the buyer has a goal in mind and a logical business case in place based on facts, on how the vendor can fit into the assortment.

There are any number of ways to approach negotiation. Experience may be the best teacher. Ultimately, you want to put yourself in a position to win. Like most good things, it takes a plan.

A Final Word on Returns

Returns and exchanges are the dark side of retail, and most merchants would rather talk about something else. Sadly, returns come with the territory, and they can be a significant drain on profitability and efficiency.

There seems to be an endless debate between retailers and suppliers regarding who should bear the responsibility for returned merchandise. The retail perspective is that a customer claims that the product is defective. People in the stores cannot dispute the claim or test a manufacturer's product. Therefore, it's the vendor's problem. A manufacturer would respond that less than one-half of 1 percent of their products are truly defective. You (the retailer) expect me to take back all these goods because of your policy, not mine. You should challenge your customers and not take back these returns. Additionally, you send me returns that are missing parts, missing the free give-away merchandise, or missing the original packaging, yet you expect full credit.

In truth, both parties need to share in this responsibility, and in the end, the consumer will ultimately pay because the price of merchandise will bear this expense. The American public has been conditioned to expect that every retailer will take back anything, no questions asked. It may have begun with the Sears policy ("Satisfaction Guaranteed or Your Money Back") over a century ago. Now, the opportunity for retailers is to provide that "satisfaction" and avoid the return and be extremely efficient with the returns that cannot be avoided.

Returns programs are generally negotiated and maintained by the merchant. As any new vendor is established, the returns policy needs to be defined. In addition, the programs for existing suppliers should be reviewed periodically (at least yearly) to ensure that they continue to be effective. As a merchandise manager, I always scrutinized return policies with any line review.

Much like allowances, return programs can come in all shapes and sizes. It's important that the buyer clearly define these policies in order to avoid discrepancies down the road. Again, retail is detail. So what do retailers do with those returns? The following are some options:

1.   Return them to the shelf. Many returns are the result of buyer's remorse. "I paid too much." "I didn't like the color when I got it home." If the goods are still in new condition and there are no packaging issues, the product may simply be sent back to stock. Examples might be towels, toys, or auto parts, and they are resold at full price.

2.   Mark it down. Often, returned merchandise is perfectly fine but doesn't look fresh. For example, a man's dress shirt that has been removed from its package. The article is new, but the pins are missing and the fold is no longer crisp. Generally these goods can be put back on the shelf at a reduced price.

3.   Return it to the vendor (RTV). It sounds simple and straightforward, but the details can be very important. Who pays the freight back to the vendor? Typically, the retailer will absorb this cost. If, however, a product is truly defective or recalled due to a defect or quality issue, the merchant should attempt to push this freight charge back to the supplier.

Another challenge can be missing parts. A calculator is returned without the adapter. A grill goes back to Sears without the cover. A vacuum cleaner is returned to Target without the instruction manual or the attachments. When the problem is small and the rate of return is minor, these omissions often fly under the radar, and the manufacturer will eat the cost. Occasionally, however, suppliers will deduct the cost of missing parts from any credit due. Return authorization (RA) can be another question when returning goods to the vendor. Some chains prefer an RA for tracking purposes while others prefer to send goods back without the hassle and delay of calling for an RA. I've also seen situations where a vendor provided a blanket RA. That is, one number that is universally used for returns.

4. Refurbish it. Some manufacturers insist on refurbishing returns. This is often seen as a solution on expensive mechanical or electronic products. Expensive shredders, a punch-'n'-bind machine, or an overhead projector might be examples of where refurbishing can apply. In this circumstance, the supplier will send the returned goods back to the retailer in "like new" condition. All packaging is replaced, manuals and parts are checked, and if anything was truly defective (it usually isn't), it is repaired.

   As a merchant, I would strongly consider changing vendors before accepting such a policy.

5. Repair it. Some products are repaired rather than taken back. This is more common with electronics or power equipment and is often employed when a customer brings back a product that is beyond the normal thirty-day window of accepting a return.

6. Liquidate it. There is always someone willing to take away obsolete or returned product for the right price. Although liquidating bad stock at ten or fifteen cents on the dollar can be painful, the alternative is worse. Hanging on to bad merchandise serves no purpose and it ties up money that could otherwise be spent on new goods.

Most retailers have avenues of liquidation or charities that will accept products.

7. Destroy it. This sounds drastic but may be the best solution. Many products just don't hold enough value to repair them, return them, restock them, or even sell off to a liquidator. If the merchant and the supplier can negotiate an allowance that will cover returns, the financial impact is (theoretically) covered.

As an example, most car-audio manufacturers would rather provide an allowance on car-audio speakers than have them returned. They ask that the retailer "crush" all returns. On some periodic basis, the retailer should check to see that the allowance covers the actual value of the returns.

The goal of any retailer should be to sell it right and keep it sold. Still, in many circumstance, returns are inevitable. A good merchant will watch returns closely as a way to monitor customer satisfaction and profitability. I always advocate that a reason for return needs to be captured so that corrective action can be taken to improve customer satisfaction. As an example, in the late '90s, return rates on digital cameras were well over 25 percent for most national retailers. By seeking a reason for return, one prominent retailer discovered that most cameras came back because the customer didn't know how to load the film. Some quick training to store associates and a packaging change reduced returns to single digits fairly quickly.

Attending a Trade Show

Most industries have trade associations which serve as a focal point for the sharing of information, lobbying on behalf of the trade, educating its members, and a host of additional activities. Often, the associations will orchestrate a trade show as a way to bring their membership together. A trade show can be a great place to gain visibility to market trends, build relationships between suppliers and retailers, and discuss business issues.

Due to the great diversity of retail, there are as many trade shows as there are categories of merchandise: COMDEX (the computer world's show), the National Hardware Show, the Housewares Show, CES (Consumer Electronic Show), the Gourmet Show, Toy Fair, SHOPA (School, Home and Office Products Association), just to name a few.

The attendees of a trade show are generally made up of a broad spectrum of people, including the exhibitors (sales reps, company staffers, and executives), buyers, trade press, and other association members. Both retailers and manufacturers, depending on their size, may send multiple levels of people to a show ranging from buyers and sales reps to key executives. As a result, communication and meetings can take place at various levels. Basically, there are three types of meetings that occur at any trade show.

1. Top-to-top meetings. The senior management of two companies meet to share strategic visions, long-range plans, and possibly discuss critical issues. The objective is often about alignment. Such meetings are not about the day-to-day interactions between the companies or about picking SKUs. Agenda items might include the following:

    - Discuss the possibility of a co-branding campaign at holiday
    - Present the company's supply chain initiative and ask for participation at specific levels
    - Review market share goals

2. Strategic meetings. Key people from the retailer (buyers, merchandise managers, merchant vice-president) meet with key players from the manufacturer or vendor to review and discuss their business together. The focus is typically on the near future. Often, this time is used to resolve problems, negotiate specific issues, and generally share industry or company insights. Agenda items for a strategic meeting might include the following:

- Review business/industry trends. Is our business plan on target?
- Our post-audit group needs a contact within the manufacturer to resolve open issues.
- Explore consignment inventory as an option to improve our in-stock position and increase sales.
- Provide an update on our website work and discuss the linkages we need from the vendor.

3. Business meetings. These meetings are primarily tactical. Such sessions address the day-to-day business issues of promotional planning, assortment selection or new item reviews, financial issues, shipping, and so forth. An agenda for the typical business meeting might include the following:

- Review sales plan to date
- Share insights on any new company priorities
- Review new products
- Discuss support needed for fall ad campaign
- Resolve invoice discrepancies

With such diverse agendas, it becomes important that preplanning and follow up be done. As a merchandise manager, I always began the prep work sixty to ninety days prior to any major show, with a discussion of the purpose in attending the show. What do we hope to accomplish? Which meetings and at what level need to be scheduled? And who should attend? This early thinking can help greatly with some of the basics such as preregistration (this can save hours of time standing in long lines at the show), hotel rooms, and schedules. In large companies where there may be numerous attendees for a specific event, it might be helpful to create a comprehensive list. For example,

Housewares Show				
Chicago – McCormick Place				
Attendee	**Arrive**	**Hotel**	**Depart**	**Cell**
John Smith, Sr. Buyer – Vacuums	6/11	Hyatt	6/14	712-555-1212
Alice Jones, MM – Floorcare	6/11	Hyatt	6/15	712-555-1213
Sue Johnson, VP, GMM	6/12	Hilton	6/14	712-555-1214
Don Sullivan, Inventory Director	6/11	Hyatt	6/13	712-555-1215
Jim Morris, Sr. Buyer - Appliances	6/12	Hilton	6/14	712-555-1216
Bill Nelson, Internet Director	6/12	Hilton	6/14	712-555-1216

This list can be shared by all team members so that everyone knows the cell number and hotel of everyone else.

Another useful tool is a simple schedule or show planner. The pace of a trade show will require that you're organized and know where you're going. Convention centers like Las Vegas or Chicago's McCormick Place can be overwhelming. Organization pays off. Perhaps the greatest pitfall in scheduling is overbooking. As a young buyer, I found that I fell into this trap quite often. Demands for my time would leave me running from one meeting to another because I failed to factor travel time into my plans. I also quickly learned that overbooking myself left me no time to casually walk the exhibits to look for new products or new ideas.

Sample Schedule Planner			
International Housewares Show—Chicago			
Sunday, March 20 through Tuesday, March 22			
	Saturday	Sunday	Monday
	March 19	March 20	March 21
7:00			
7:30		Breakfast w/team	
8:00			Breakfast w/Hoover, Marriott Hotel
8:30			
9:00		Arrow Plastic Booth 1012	

Time			
9:30			Hoover Booth 2100
10:00		Newall Booth 2216	
10:30			
11:00	NWA Flight 21		
11:30	Depart MSP 11:10		
12:00	Arrive ORD 12:30	Mr. Coffee Booth 715	Eureka (Lunch) Booth 2606
12:30	Hotel Info:		
1:00	The W Hotel on Lake Shore Dr	HoMedics Booth 680	Walk Show
1:30	at Ontario 312-456-7890		
2:00		Braun (Shavers) Booth 740	Walk show
2:30			
3:00		Panasonic (Shavers) Booth 930	Walk show
3:30			
4:00		Norelco (Shavers) Booth 946	Sharp Booth 2515
4:30			
5:00			
5:30			
Evening	7:00 PM Dinner with Rubbermaid – meet at Rosebuds 312-456-7890 John Smith, SVP	7:00 PM Dinner with Salton – Lawrey's, State and Ontario, Bob White, VP of Sales	Depart for Airport NWA, Flight. 26 Depart ORD 7:15 Arrive MSP 8:45

Schedule Notes:

1.   A good planner begins and ends with travel information and accounts for the time in between.
2.   Try to group your meetings sensibly to prevent downtime. In a large convention hall, you may walk many miles in a day. Grouping meetings by general location will save your legs and your time. Note the groupings of floorcare vendors on day 2 (Monday) as an example.
3.   Add details that will enhance your efficiency. For instance, names of people you'll meet, phone numbers in the event you're running late, booth numbers, and so forth.

4. Schedule time to walk the show. If you don't, chances are you'll miss it.

Behind every planner is an agenda for each vendor meeting. Each agenda should include the following elements:

- Date, time, and location of the meeting
- Attendees and their titles (both retailer and vendor)
- Cellphone numbers are often helpful
- Agenda items
- If a presentation is being done, will A/V equipment be needed?
- Space for notes. This can become a working document.

The schedule and all meeting agendas can be placed in a binder or portfolio to create a "show book." I've known buyers that will add SKU listings, ad plans, and vendor programs to their show book as a way to have details readily available. However you add to it, the show book becomes your tool to stay on time and remain focused on key objectives.

Post Mortem

As a general rule, I always expect a post mortem or debrief from trade-show attendees. Gaining their insights can help to gauge the show's importance (should we attend next year?). Additionally, a debrief helps me to understand if objectives were achieved, and it gives me a line of sight to any action items or issues for follow up. Such recaps can be kept simple. Take the following for example:

Overview

The Housewares Show broke all attendance records, and the biggest story was color. From plastic to coffee makers, most manufactures were showing multiple colors of their products.

John Smith was a powerful keynote speaker. He emphasized the shift of business toward Internet retailers . . . .

Vendor-by-Vendor Synopsis

1. Acme Oven Mitt Company—Met with senior sales exec to discuss improved payment terms. We're looking for an additional fifteen days. They will respond by end of month.
2. Best Company—We explained the need to reduce their assortment due to space limitations. They agreed to support a markdown for store merchandise, and we'll maintain the offering on the website.

Action Items

1. Have samples of Jones Company blenders sent to the photo studio
2. Send new vendor packages to XYZ company, QRS Company, and LMN Company
3. Advise accounting to write off the debit balance of Smith, Inc.
4. Follow up on signed MDF agreements

If attending a trade show is starting to sound like work, it is. A successful trip requires preplanning, a solid schedule, and follow up after the show. Still, it's also a time to build relationships. Be sure to take the time for fun or a dinner that's not all business.

Chapter Eleven

THE LINE REVIEW

The term "line review" in retail merchandising is not about models walking the runway wearing the latest fashions. It's really about knowing that the buyer actually has a firm grasp on his business. It's an important part of any retail organization and serves multiple purposes.

1. Blocking and tackling: It's a quick review to be sure that the basic merchant building blocks are in place.

2. Alignment: It's an opportunity to ensure that all parties associated with a product category understand and are aligned around the strategic direction and positioning within the company.

3. Forum for input: Depending on the audience, the line review can often be used as a forum for the various disciplines to express concerns or explain unique variables that may need consideration. Often, a "different" set of eyes can lead to enhancement of an assortment.

4. Opportunities: This exercise will always identify areas of opportunity.

5. Set priorities: It's a way to communicate to the entire team what the priorities are and how they will be addressed. When support groups are privy to the big picture, it's much easier to see the value of their work and how they fit in.

Over the years, I have conducted, participated in, and delivered line reviews on numerous product categories in several industries. While there have always been common practices, there have also been variables based on the industry, the type of product, or the company format. The following pages will describe what I believe to be the most critical pieces of any line review. Note, however, that methods and specifics will vary from one situation to the next. Still, I think you'll "get it." The explanation will be followed by an example that should further illustrate the process.

Elements of the Line Review

Audience

The audience may vary from one (the boss) to many. I have always thought of this activity as an event that can be a good forum to hear from support teams like marketing, inventory, space management, accounting, and others, as well as a way to align the broader team around the goals and expectations of the category. Larger organizations will often use the line review as a presentation to senior management. It keeps them in touch with the business and allows for their experience to provide improved direction. Whatever your approach, be sure to invite people well in advance and be clear on any preparation or contributions they need to make.

Definition

Any line review must begin with a clear definition of the business being reviewed. For example, digital cameras, category 123 / all subcategories, greeting cards, or shampoos.

The role and intent or category strategy should be stated up front as well. Additionally, other information that may help to frame up the discussion would typically be stated up front. Examples might be sales volume (LY vs. TY), overall gross margin, budget, number of resets per year, and so forth.

Category Vision

Where do you want to see this category in eighteen months to three years? This statement should literally paint the picture. When working on BestBuy.com many years ago, our "vision" for digital imaging was to be the "helpful friend" that could guide the consumer into the camera solution that would best meet his/her needs based on lifestyle. The site would offer tips in photography. Services would be available to safeguard your imagery, offer storage capacity, and make prints available via mail, in-store pickup, or at home using a personal photo printer. The site would have applications to enhance your photos, put a mustache on grandma, or share. Our aim was to build a community, not just sell cameras with flash memory. Again, this was the vision. You still cannot do some of these things on BestBuy.com. A vision is what you strive to be. It's aspirational.

Vendor Data

The most basic building block of vendor data is an essential step to any line review. This is simply a list of all vendors, key contacts, mailing addresses, phone numbers, cell phone numbers, and e-mail addresses.

Now, one might think that such information would readably reside in the "system" and that this modest exercise seems like a waste of time. From experience, I can tell you that it is vital. Surprisingly, most retailers cannot produce such a list. I have often asked or been asked to advise all vendors of some important information only to discover that a simple mailing requires the buyers to scramble and pull together a list of vendors. With no central repository for the information, this exercise would be requested again and again. Then, of course, often we would have bad information like a representative who hadn't represented a particular company in years, yet they are still on someone's list. On more than one occasion, I reviewed this data and found a key contact listed that was actually dead (true story).

Program Review

Vendor deals and programs are thoroughly explained in the chapter on allowances. Any line review must include a recap of the programs (programs being things like payment terms, freight terms, returns allowances, cooperative advertising allowances, volume incentives, and so forth) for all vendors associated with the product category being reviewed. Without this recap, a true picture of profitability by vendor is impossible.

When programs are recapped and reviewed by category, it's often easy to spot opportunities or probe areas that appear questionable. Some examples that I have lived through are the following:

1.   While looking over this part of a line review on audio products, I saw that every vendor had terms of Net 60 except one. The exception had payment terms of Net 30. So why is there one vendor below par on terms? In truth, the buyer never looked at all of his programs lined up in order and was simply not aware of the anomaly. One phone call pushed those terms to Net 60.

2.   I once reviewed furniture in a retail environment in which the category was very minor. In fact, the total SKU count was thirty. When looking at a list of programs for nine vendors, it was immediately obvious that we needed to consolidate. Sharing thirty SKUs amongst nine suppliers gives you very little leverage and adds cost. We consolidated to using three suppliers, become a meaningful customer to those three, and improved our programs with each as a result of the added volume.

3.   Many times I have stumbled upon odd or hard-to-collect allowances that become clearly visible as the programs were lined up. One example was a 2-percent volume allowance on all purchases in excess of $5 million. Our volume had been about $4 million for three years in a row. The allowances looked good, but we never received it. The 2 percent was renegotiated into the cost of goods sold.

Supply Chain and Vendor Performance Metrics

What are the important measures of vendor performance? The best cost in the world doesn't mean very much if the vendor cannot fill your orders. So what matters to your company?

In-Stock

Many companies will measure the "in-stock" level by vendor. Defining "in-stock" can be tricky. Is it having one piece of each SKU in every store? Is it having one piece in addition to the display? Is it having one piece of sellable inventory (not a returned product or display unit)? Is it having one available for sale unit at each planogrammed location (many items are merchandised in multiple locations? Examples may be candies, sodas, or batteries)? Is it having two days worth of sales in available inventory?

However it is measured, if applied consistently to all vendors and products, it provides a barometer for reviewing performance.

Lead time

This is often an indicator of performance. A shorter lead time typically improves inventory turn and reduces safety stock. This metric is commonly defined as the average number of days from order placement to the actual receipt of the goods.

Days of Supply (DOS)

The number of days that would be required to sell through all the inventory of a vendor.

Shipping Performance

Are the goods shipped on time and are the orders filled completely? Vendors that ship multiple times against a single purchase order are prone to back orders or are late with shipments add cost to the retailer.

Compliance

Often a retailer will have specific shipping criteria in place in order to improve costs or efficiency. Examples might be preferred carriers, carton label instructions for ease of identification, or pallet specification for efficient movement within their system. Is the vendor complying with these requirements?

Electronic Data Interchange (EDI)

Is the supplier compliant and timely with all EDI communication? This can include advance shipping notices, packing lists, and other exchanges of information.

Inventory Turnover

What's the turn rate of the category being reviewed? Depending on the available data turn by vendor within the category can be a good metric to identify opportunities.

Industry Review

What's the state of the industry concerning this category? A trend toward designer hair care products is important to know. Music sales decline as MP3 players gain momentum. Factories have closed due to commoditization, leaving fewer choices for your assortment.

As a merchant, I have seen countless trends unfold that had profound impacts on sourcing or product decisions. Some examples are the following:

1. Typewriters gave way to word processors that gave way to computers. Has anyone purchased a ball element or correction tape for a Selectric III typewriter lately?
2. Paper has become a commodity product. Copy paper will have pricing fluctuations based on mill capacity versus demand. In a tight market, there is upward pressure on price, and it can often be difficult to ensure a steady supply. Conversely, if a new mill is scheduled to come online, you might anticipate a softer market, greater availability, and lower prices.
3. Grocery trends serve as a good example of how the merchant needs to be in touch with the industry. The Atkins diet

spawned changes in demand for salty snacks, breads (more rye and whole grains, less white), and prepared foods. The industry responded to the speed of society and more working moms with more prepared meals.

Item Level Review

A SKU by SKU review of the category will require some reporting. Typically, this is a SKU (product) listing with multiple views. First, items are ranked in descending order of sales velocity; key elements include: UPC, model number, product description, unit of measure (is it sold in dozens, packs, or eaches?), retail price, unit cost, gross margin, number of units sold, total sales volume, and total gross margin. These metrics can be gathered for a specific time period and year-to-date rollups.

Another view of this data might be a rollup by vendor. Yet another might be listing the SKUs in price point order. Each view is intended to help the merchant understand what sells and what doesn't.

Ad Plans

The line review is the perfect opportunity to review ad plans. I have always asked that buyers incorporate their ad checkerboard for a forward look as well as current or past ads. It's an opportunity to verify that the ad strategy aligns with the category strategy.

Additionally, ads should be reviewed for a period of time. Look for efficient use of space, accuracy of sale stories or savings claims, results (did the advertised items produce?), changes made during the process (changes are expensive), and accuracy of forecasting.

SWOT Analysis

A two by two with the quadrants labeled Strengths, Weaknesses, Opportunities, and Threats. This serves as a synopsis to understand what is really good or working, what's not, competitive issues, and so forth.

Planogram/Display

A good action step for any line review is a visual inspection of the product on display. Often this is an in-store visit or an actual mock-up done at the corporate office. Things to look for:

1. Will the display hold sales? Based on sales velocity, are there enough positions (pegs or shelf space) to support the sales of the product? On many occasions, I have found a substantial sales increase just through adjusting the space on a planogram. If, for example, your rate of sale for an item is twenty per store per week and there are two pegs that can hold three pieces each (six total), there may be an opportunity. At a minimum, labor is being spent to restock those pegs three to four times a week. Also, it's likely that sales are being stifled.

2. Packaging. Often a visual inspection can present opportunities in packaging. I've seen package changes occur that the buyer wasn't aware of. I've seen illogical adjacencies. I've seen bland packages that could benefit from feature and benefit callouts, better color, or a clamshell instead of cardboard. Once, during a line review of phones, the physical inspection at a store turned up a line of pay-as-you-go phones in clamshell packaging that were too heavy for the package. This resulted in the eye (the hole used to hang it on a peg) breaking. The store was reinforcing every piece of product with duct tape so that it would not fall off the hook. A quick call to the vendor fixed the problem, but it might have gone on for a long time had it not been for the line review.

3. Signage. Does the signage properly support the display? Is informational signage in place? Shelf tags will vary by retailer, but typically a tag will show the retail price, the unit of measure (each, dozen, pack, etc.), a UPC (Universal Product Code) number, and possibly a replenishment code.

Competition

Who is the competition? How do they treat the category? Advertise the category? Price the products? Are there new competitive threats to consider?

Internet

If the retailer has a commercial Internet site, it too needs to be a part of the line review process. Because the Internet is a different channel, there may be implications to the assortment, prices, even the strategy for this category.

Example of a Line Review

To make this topic real, I've selected a product category that can be found in grocery stores, office products stores, mass market stores, drug, electronics, hardware, and many other venues . . . batteries. Although the elements and information may change depending on the environment, I believe the example provides a good view of the process. Of course, the information that follows is pure fiction. The process begins by setting up the day or time in advance.

To: Merchandise Managers, Buyers, and Inventory Analysts
          Other Associates that drive the category
From: The Reviewing Party (usually Merchant VP)
Subject: Battery Line Review
Date: Month, Date, Year

A line review of the battery category has been scheduled for Monday. Please think of this as your day as well as mine. It's an opportunity to get grounded in your business and for leadership to better understand the product category.

Agenda:

8:00-9:00 a.m.	Overview/Basics 1. Category role, intent, and vision 2. Vendor data—key contacts 3. Vendor data—programs and deals 4. Vendor data—debit balances, credit holds
9:00-10:00 a.m.	External Factors 1. Industry insight 2. Competition 3. SWOT Synopsis
10:00-11:00 a.m.	Assortment/Performance 1. SKU listing review 2. Performance to plan/budget 3. Supply chain performance metrics
11:00-2:00 p.m.	Market Visit and Lunch Walk the store Visit key competitors
2:00-3:00 p.m.	Promotional Planning 1. Review checkerboard (3-6 month look) 2. TY vs. LY performance/space/week 3. Ad review—key events, competition
3:00-5:00 p.m.	Open discussion • Private label business within the category • Planograms—visually appealing? How many resets per year? • Packaging opportunities • Dot com. Does the site align with stores? • Direct marketing, off-shelf displays • Resources needed to meet plan • Feedback on the day

This agenda sets the review in motion. The buyer is then responsible to pull the required information together and present it. That presentation might look like the following:

Line Review

Batteries

1

Line Review - Batteries

Vision

To be a key contributor to both sales and gross margin by establishing XYZ Retail as an authority on batteries and thru improved attachment rates to products that use them.

2

Industry View – Battery Highlights

The battery category generates over $4B annually!

✓Category is growing **7% this year**
✓Opportunities to generate high margin

3

Industry View – Battery Highlights

The Battery Category Generates $4.2 Billion Annually

$3.78B

Household

• Includes all standard cell sizes (AA, AAA, C, D, 9V)

$420MM

Specialty

• All non-standard cell sizes

Specialty
10%

Household
90%

4

Line Review - Batteries

Battery Industry

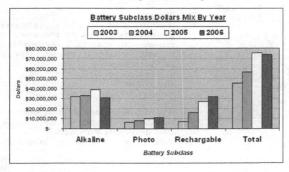

5

Line Review - Batteries

Battery Industry Brand Share

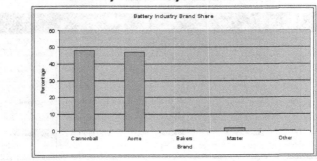

6

Line Review - Batteries

Focus

1. Dominant assortment
2. Merchandise batteries in the right places to gain convenience sales and attachments while controlling inventory. Cross-merchandise with clip strips: use shippers in holiday season; permanent placement at check lanes
3. Reduce slow moving sku's. In Premium Alkaline segment - 10 skus produce 50% of the business. In Photo - 10 skus produce 90% of the business.
4. Prepare disaster plans. Build capability to immediately ship pallets to natural disaster areas (hurricanes and floods).
5. Maintain brand assortment on dot.com site.

Line Review - Batteries

Vendor Contacts

Vendor	Vendor #	Key Contact	Contact Address	Phone	E-mail
Acme Battery	006	John Doe	Acme Building, 400 N. Broadway, Madison WI 53202	414-231-1244	john@acme.com
Bakers Specialty	121	Jane Doe	5200 Wilson Road, Edina, MN 55439	612-456-7890	jane@baker.com
Canonball Battery	226	Bill Smith	PO Box 5722, Oak Park, IL 60302	312-789-0123	bill@canonball.com
Illinois Industrial	357	Harold Brown	222 Baker Street, Bongbrook, IL 60440	630-456-7890	harold@ill.com
Master Battery	408	Anita Jones	356 Adams Street, Atlanta, GA 31146	404-781-2250	anita@master.com
Solutions	521	Felix Lopez	19000 Riverside, San Antonio, TX 55412	512-889-6730	felix@solution.com
Venture	617	Howard Kramer	44 Park Place, New York, NY 11042	216-344-8811	howard@venture.com

Line Review - Batteries

Vendor Programs

Vendor	Vend #	Payment Terms	Freight Terms	Allowances			Returns	Comments
				New Store	Coop	Other		
Acme	006	Net 60	Prepaid	Free pallet of product	5% QBB		1% MBB Destroy in Field	QBB = Quartrbill back MBB = Monthly
Bakers	121	Net 60	Prepaid	1st Order free	6% QBB	2% Annual Volume	No Policy	
Cannonball	357	Consignment	Prepaid	$1500 per store	5% MBB		Call for excessive returns	Extended terms in Q4
Master	408	Net 75	Prepaid	25% off	7% QBB	$50K MDF	No Policy	
Solutions	521	Net 30	Prepaid	-	-	-	No Policy	Private Label Vendor
Venture	617	2% 60N61	Prepaid	$1000/store	10% QBB	-	2% MBB Destroy in field	

9

Line Review - Batteries

Strengths

- All Top Brands
- Private label at 25% share
- Special pallet packs at Christmas
- Cross promotions with Movies

Weaknesses

- Rechargeables not growing at industry rates
- Signage to explain benefits of rechargeables

Opportunities

- Bulk Packs
- Cross Merch with CD players
- Car Chargers for rechargeables
- Price Optimization
- Consignment Vendor – move to N75 terms
- Signage to explain benefits of rechargeables

Threats

- Big Mart advertises weekly
- Key Vendor in financial trouble: May pull co-op.
- Dead inventory clogging open to buy

10

Sku Listing - Batteries

Item#	MOD#	VENDOR	SKU_DESCRIPTION	UNIT RANK	UNIT SALES	UNIT %	RETAIL REV	GM$	GM%	WKS OF SUP	UNIT COST	UNIT RETAIL
13227	1-AA-8	Acme Battery	AA8-PACK	1	18,120	8.9%	$106,183	$49,648	30.0%	9	$4.10	$5.86
12337	2-AA-16	Acme Battery	AA16-PACK	3	10,156	5.0%	$111,008	$31,337	28.2%	10	$7.84	$10.98
00010	AAA-8	Cannonball	AAA8-PACK	4	7,864	3.8%	$54,628	$20,428	37.4%	10	$4.35	$6.49
14557	3-AA-4	Acme Battery	AA4-PACK	5	7,238	3.5%	$35,930	$17,283	48.1%	9	$2.58	$4.98
00020	AAA4	Cannonball	AAA4-PACK	6	6,943	3.4%	$34,375	$17,348	50.5%	11	$2.45	$4.49
10000	9V-2	Venture	9V2-PACK	8	6,808	3.3%	$45,293	$12,104	26.7%	11	$4.87	$6.79
00030	AA-16	Cannonball	AA16 PACK	9	6,732	3.3%	$73,283	$22,917	31.3%	19	$7.48	$10.49
4100	AAA8	Master	AAA8-PACK	10	6,889	3.3%	$43,059	$10,726	24.9%	14	$4.83	$6.99
20000	AA-4	Venture	AA4-PACK	11	6,261	3.1%	$31,047	$15,781	50.8%	11	$2.45	$4.79
1-1000	AA-8	Bakers	AA8 PACK	12	6,149	3.0%	$54,883	$18,212	33.2%	13	$5.96	$8.99
4200	AA-8	Master	AA SIZE 8-PK	13	5,476	2.7%	$23,679	$18,855	42.5%	16	$3.10	$5.49
1-2000	AAA4	Bakers	AAA4-PACK	14	5,349	2.6%	$26,483	$12,730	48.1%	14	$2.57	$5.39
13227	9-V2	Acme Battery	9V2-PACK	16	5,300	2.6%	$34,494	$10,598	30.7%	16	$4.51	$6.98
00040	AA-20	Cannonball	AA20PK DOUBLEWIDE	19	4,876	2.4%	$60,685	$10,306	17.0%	5	$10.33	$12.49
4300	D-4	Master	D-4 PACK	20	4,737	2.3%	$17,990	$9,193	51.1%	26	$1.86	$5.99
15667	5-AA-4	Acme Battery	AA4 PACK ULTRA	21	4,720	2.3%	$28,120	$13,307	47.3%	15	$3.14	$5.98
4400	AAA16	Master	AAA 16-PACK	22	4,659	2.3%	$50,859	$14,939	29.4%	22	$7.71	$10.99
00050	AA-48	Cannonball	AA SIZE 48-PK	24	4,181	2.0%	$39,003	$18,425	47.2%	12	$4.92	$20.49
30000	MAXD-8	Venture	MAX D-8 DOUBLE WIDE	26	3,854	1.9%	$41,839	$12,554	30.0%	5	$7.60	$10.79

11

Line Review Batteries

Supply Chain Metrics

Batteries	In Stock			On Time Receipt			Total Lead Time			Inventory Turnover		
	TY	LY	% Change	TY	LY	% Change	TY	LY	% Change	TY	LY	% Change
Acme	91.42%	87.89%	4.01%	88.59%	89.49%	-1.01%	16.7	17.3	-3.76%	6.8	6.4	.4
Bakers	92.19%	86.65%	6.40%	79.20%	63.65%	24.43%	16.5	17.9	-7.83%	7.1	7.0	.1
Cannonball	94.02%	93.84%	0.19%	62.01%	83.90%	-26.09%	9.9	10.9	-9.26%	6.5	6.5	-
Master	92.24%	86.07%	6.39%	70.54%	59.16%	19.07%	16.0	16.2	-1.72%	4.5	4.0	.5
Venture	94.46%	91.45%	3.28%	84.71%	83.08%	1.96%	15.5	15.3	1.04%	6.8	6.2	.6
Totals	92.21%	87.13%	5.83%	79.78%	74.89%	6.53%	15.3	16.6	-7.61	6.6	6.1	.5

12

Ad Plan - Batteries

Battery	June Mailer	July Insert	August Insert	August Mailer	Sept Insert	Oct Insert
Acme AA 4 Pk	X		X			X
Acme AAA 4 Pk	X		X			X
Acme C 4 Pk	X		X			X
Acme D 4 Pk	X		X			X
Acme AV 2 Pk	X		X			X
Acme AA Bulk Pk				X		
Canonball AA 4 Pk		X			X	X
Canonball AAA 4 Pk		X			X	X
Canonball C 4 Pk		X			X	X
Canonball D 4 Pk		X			X	X
Canonball 9V 2 Pk		X			X	
Private Label AA		X				X
Private Label AAA		X				X
Private Label C		X				X
Private Label D		X				X
Private Label Bulk AA		X				
Photo Batteries			X			
	Special $1 off Coupon	Your Choice	Buy 2 Get 1 Free Sale	Bulk Savings	Anniversary Sale – Event 25% off	Good Better Best Choice

13

Line Review - Batteries

For Discussion:

- Increase private label sales
- Drive rechargeables
- Introduce side caps in key areas
- Reduce promotions to save gross margin
- Drop low performing vendor?

14

Elements of the line review process will vary by industry and by category. If the objective is to thoroughly understand the business and identify opportunities for improvement, it's necessary to be flexible. At Quill Corporation and other mail-order or Internet companies, the case pack, inner pack, and weights are critical because everything is shipped to consumers. The display or packaging demands of Williams-Sonoma are much different from the Home Depot store. The key is to do line reviews. It will almost always add to the bottom line.

Chapter Twelve

THE GREAT MERCHANT

The truly great merchant is a special blend of passion and reason wrapped in a cloak of solid ethical behavior.

While this topic steps away from the central theme of blocking 'n' tackling, I believe it is far too important to neglect. To explain this challenging topic, I have separated the "ethics" from the "reason" and "passion" pieces. By focusing on these pieces, I hope that each will compliment the other and leave the reader with an understanding of the whole—the great merchant.

A Matter of Ethics

Perhaps the most difficult lesson to teach young buyers is the balance that is needed in vendor relationships. I firmly believe that business friendships and relationships can aid communication and build a trust that can help both retailer and manufacturer move the business forward together. There is, however, an invisible line that must always exist between the buyer and the seller. It's a line of ethics. If crossed, it can lead a buyer to put his self-interests ahead of his employers'. It can often create a sense of obligation toward the vendor, which may cloud his thinking on business issues.

So, where's the line and who's the best judge of when it's crossed? It's a hard concept to explain. It's about a round of golf or taking in a baseball game with a vendor and getting to know people on a personal level. There is a great deal of good in this. But the next morning, it's business again. Knowing that Sally's children get their braces off on

Wednesday is no reason to add a SKU or place an order with Sally. The merchant needs to remain fact based and return to his tenacious self after the game.

The power of the pen brings with it a tremendous responsibility. I recall Bob Theer, a former Sears merchant, once telling me that the "power" actually created a little fear at times. When Sears would add or drop a few SKUs, it could make or ruin the bonuses for everyone at a manufacturer. In fact, if Sears were 50% of your business, a change could put you out of business. This same power can play on the integrity or ethics of the business relationship. Think about a sales rep that depends upon the merchant for ten million dollars in business. Or how about $100 million worth of orders? Is that worth a few tickets to the football game? Not a big deal. Or is it worth a weekend at a prestigious golf resort in Arizona? What about some cash?

Ethics is a delicate, complicated subject that doesn't always fit into neat black-and-white explanations. Through the course of twenty-five years in the merchant role, I have seen and been confronted with ethical tests many times. Some of those stories may help to add context to this topic. These tales are all true.

Take the Money, Harvey

The first trade show that I ever attended was the NOPA (National Office Products Association) show in Chicago. I was a rebuyer for Quill Corporation at the time and was truly in awe of my first look at massive show displays and an entire industry coming together in one place. In those days, it was not uncommon for vendors to write orders at the show. Small dealers often took advantage of show specials to beef up their bottom line. Although Quill was no small dealer, I had prepared several orders just in case there was an opportunity to take advantage of a deal. At the Louis Melind booth, such an opportunity presented itself.

Melind was a small manufacturer of rubber stamps and inks. Their convention special was 10% off any order placed at the show. I handed the rep an order for $2000 and noted that we would receive 10% off on my copy of the purchase order. When I looked up, the sales rep was shoving $200 in cash into my hand. Cash! "Here's your ten percent off," was all he said. I left the booth literally in a sweat. How did this look? What if someone saw me taking cash from a vendor?

About fifteen minutes later, I ran into Harvey Miller down another aisle. Harvey was one of the owners of Quill. I explained what had happened and handed the cash to him. That two hundred bucks was one of the heaviest burdens I ever carried.

Ethics? A cash incentive was this vendor's way of driving business. Many of the show attendees were owner/operators of independent stationery stores. Cash was acceptable to an owner (I wonder if they declared the income). As for purchasing agents, they faced the same dilemma that I did. Each made his own choice.

Who the Hell Are You?

This one is as hilarious as it is unethical. My director of alcoholic beverage for a drug-store chain told me this story. A key executive with the company was going to Las Vegas and wanted good seats for the big fight at Caesars. This was the hottest ticket in town, and he had to really lean on the local liquor distributor to get two $500 seats.

As it turned out, the supplier had four seats near ringside. He gave up two for the executive and used the other two for himself and another client. Before the big fight, he turned to the two guys seated to his left and said, "So, how do you like these seats?"

The man responded, "Oh yeah. Great, pal." The vendor, not one to be put off, said, "Well, I'm Bill Smith with ABC Distributing. We arranged for the seats. I'm glad you like them."

The man to his left looked confused but responded, "What are you talkin' about? And who the hell are you? I bought these tickets from a guy out front for $600 a piece about an hour ago."

Yes, our executive sold the seats, made a profit, and stayed at the craps table rather than go to the fight. That one strained the vendor relationship a little.

Dinner for Two

Same company, different executive. The boss called me to his office. "Hey, Danny"—in this company, everyone was Danny, Joey, Billy, or Suzie. It was a local thing—"I'll be in Chicago on Thursday night. See if you can set me up with dinner for two at Lawry's."

To clarify, I asked if he meant that I should set up a vendor dinner. If so, which vendor? The answer was "no." He wanted me to arrange for a vendor to simply leave a credit card at the restaurant. He and a friend would dine. The bill goes on the credit card.

I never made a call, and thankfully, the executive never brought it back up to me.

We'll Pay for Our Own Holiday Party

As companies evolve from small start-up positions to midsize to large, the emphasis on ethical behavior often grows. What may have been perfectly acceptable in an owner/operator state is far too "grey" when thousands of employees are expected to know where to begin and end regarding supplier relationships.

I saw this transformation in several of the companies I worked for. At one such company, it had become common practice to throw a nice holiday party for the marketing team. This was a very nice affair with spouses, an open bar, entertainment, and a great meal. Of course, it was pricey too.

Each year, the merchants were asked to line up several sponsors. That is, arrange for a few of the local rep groups to pick up the tab. Then one year, a change in management occurred. It occurred at a point where the growth of the company really made this practice of hitting up the reps something that now seemed out of line. The new guy recognized that we had outgrown such practice as a company. If we expected to stand tall on the ethics and values that we tried to instill in our people, this had to stop. I applauded the change. There was no steak at the holiday party that year.

A Win for Charity

I once served as the merchandise manager for a broad category of general merchandise. Included in the assortment were electric shavers. As I sat in on a vendor meeting one day, the salesman asked me to please take a shaver for my personal use. As it turned out, I was in the market for a new shaver but knew that I couldn't simply accept a $100 sample.

Well, the salesman argued that it was important that I understand how this product is differentiated from others. His company believes that their customers need to use the product to understand it and to sell it to our customers with conviction.

I offered to pay for it, but he wouldn't accept any money. Finally, my boss gave me an idea. He suggested that I accept the sample. If the vendor would not accept money, would he be open to a donation being made to a company-sponsored charity? He feels good. My conscience is clear, and I really do learn more about the product. That's exactly what I did.

Clouded Judgment

When the president of a medium-sized fast-growing superstore chain called to offer me a position as a merchandise manager, my first reaction was to ask which product lines I'd be responsible to oversee. He didn't answer. He believed that my breadth of experience and my merchant skills qualified me for any category and asked that I join the company without a specific category assignment.

After ten days on the job, the boss took me to dinner and explained our awkward beginning. He would be terminating another merchandise manager in the morning. It seems that the fellow had a drug problem. His connection was thought to be a manufacturer's rep that called on the company.

The chair that I inherited was in turmoil. Most vendors didn't want to deal with the company because of the unscrupulous way we had been handling the business. It seems that new vendors always needed a new rep. That rep had to be (I'll call him) Mr. Smith. A quick review of the business revealed that 80% of the volume (then about $160 million) was represented by Mr. Smith. How about 5% on $128 million? It seems that NEED met OPPORTUNITY, and the result was that a talented merchant with a family was put out of work and will probably never work in such a role again.

You Can Bet On It

Las Vegas plays host to some of the nation's largest trade shows. The city has an excellent convention center, airfares are cheap, hotels are reasonable, and the entertainment is nonstop. The Consumer Electronic Show has settled on Las Vegas as home, and every January, the industry gathers there to celebrate, exhibit, and plan for the year ahead. It was during the CES event several years ago that I had the following experience.

While walking and working the floor of the show, I ran into Leonard. Leonard was the president of one of the suppliers that I was doing business with. I had known him for several years, but we had never really had the opportunity to build the relationship. His company was relatively minor to my company's business even though our volume made us one of his largest customers. Well, Leonard kept pushing me to meet for drinks after the show, and I thought it might be good to get to know him better. I had dinner plans, so we agreed to meet at the Hilton about ten (we were both staying at the Hilton).

When I caught up with Lenny later that evening, he was accompanied by an Asian gentleman that he introduced as Mr. K. Mr. K was the owner of a factory where Lenny had his speakers produced. He was also a high roller. Before long, we were standing together at a craps table, and the two of them were throwing down big bucks amid the noise and excitement of a Vegas casino. I was enjoying the atmosphere, sipping a beer, and screaming with every roll of the dice. I was not, however, gambling. Craps is a game that moves quickly, and I'm simply not one to gamble. I work too hard for my money to see it go to the Las Vegas electric bills.

Before long, Leonard noticed that I wasn't gambling, and he placed a stack of chips on the rail in front of me saying, "C'mon, have some fun." I looked at the chips below me. It appeared to be about a thousand dollars. I slid them back to Leonard's stack. "You go ahead," I said. "I'm fine watching you. Besides, I wouldn't even know how to bet on this."

Well, Leonard wouldn't hear of it. Back came the chips. "Don't worry about it. I'll teach you. You keep whatever you win." He tossed fifty dollars onto the pass line and continued, "Here. That's your money. I'll show you how to bet and tell you when you win."

Again I slid the chips back to Leonard. "No," I repeated firmly. "I cannot gamble with your money. Don't even suggest it again." I gazed around the table and the room. It occurred to me that someone could be watching. What if another supplier, a rep, one of our buyers, or some other colleague saw Leonard pushing chips at me at the craps table? I knew nothing underhanded would occur, but could another misinterpret this? Well, as you probably suspected, Leonard pushed the chips in front of me a third time. I simply said, "Good night," left the table, and left the casino.

My relationship with Leonard has always been strictly business, and the brief foray into getting to know him better only put me on my guard. If he would come on to me in this fashion, he'd certainly come on to others, and I worried about how easily a younger buyer might fall prey to this behavior. After all the math and science, the personal relationship still matters in business. My trust is Leonard had been compromised. A year later, his business was about half of what it had been.

As I reflect on this story, the ethical lesson is significant. What if I really enjoyed gambling? What if I had had one too many drinks that night? What if the mentors I had admired and learned from had shown me through their action that a little "acceptance" was OK? I wonder about the young buyers and inventory analysts that don't have the level of experience to guide them through the grey.

Look in the Drawer

Once upon a time, there was a small chain of office products stores in Florida which was owned by a very large Canadian paper company. The chain of ten stores did about $30 million in volume, while the parent had total sales in the billions. The common joke was that the Canadians bought the company just to have a reason to travel to Florida in the winter.

It was the late '80s, and the industry was booming as superstores like Office Depot and Staples were growing and advertising with aggression. Although faced with stiff competition, the small chain continued to thrive. The Canadian parent, however, saw the future, and it was filled with Office Depot stores. They decided to sell their minor investment.

The management team put together a plan to buy the company, and the seller agreed to some very favorable terms. A date was set for the sale, and all parties seemed quite pleased. Employees would keep their jobs. Customers would never see any change. During the thirty days prior to closing the deal, however, one of the executives got greedy. He literally held a number of allowance payments from vendors in his drawer. By not cashing these checks, the final audit would undoubtedly miss them. After the sale was complete, a quick several hundred thousand dollars could be put in the bank.

I was no longer associated with the company at this time, but I had been a part of that management group. They were friends as well as associates. Well, prior to the closing, the financial officer blew the whistle. He saw his fiduciary responsibility, and he lived up to it. The result was disastrous. The Canadian responsible for the division into which this company fell took a trip to Florida. And it wasn't wintertime. Note that a $30 million company is simply a rounding error within a $10 billion enterprise. He told the operations exec to call every store and have them lock the door. The company president was dismissed, and the stores began a GOB (Going Out of Business) sale three days later. A twenty-five-year-old company with four hundred employees was gone in six weeks.

A lesson in ethics? The money would not have been material to the success or failure of the new company. What courage is needed to do the right thing as the financial executive did here? How impactful can the poor judgment of one man be?

Fore

Occasionally, I am asked to golf with a vendor or a local rep. I love the game, so I do accept the invitations once in a while. It's an opportunity to build the relationship, educate a vendor on what's important to my company, and I usually gain some great insights or ideas from just kicking it around with knowledgeable people in the industry. On the vendor side, there's an opportunity to build the bond and often learn how to better serve their customers. Four hours in the fresh air where you can be casual, is vastly different than the one-hour business meeting with a strict agenda and a clock ticking. There can be some real wins in golfing.

Some years ago, one of the local rep groups was a bit too forthcoming with invitations and opportunities to bond. In some ways, they preyed on the younger, less-seasoned people in my group, and I sensed that good judgment was being tested. This situation finally bubbled over when I learned that one of the younger people on the team was out in Las Vegas golfing with the local rep for the weekend. He was fired on Monday.

On Tuesday, I called every manufacturer that was represented by that group and suggested that they needed either no rep or a new one.

Fill 'em Up Again

A little after work, social hour can be a lot of fun. Whenever possible, I will stop in and let the team know that even the older guy can have fun. I usually don't stay too long. A former mentor once coached me that the boss will make people just a little bit uncomfortable in a social setting. Leave early so that people can let down their guard and have a good time.

On one such occasion, the crowd was mixed with a few of the local reps. Call it body language, call it instinct, but I soon realized that the reps were there for one very good reason: to pick up the tab.

It wasn't long before I noticed the waitress moving toward the group with a bill in her hand. The rep intercepted her and grabbed the check before anyone could make a move. Then I surprised the rep by taking the check away from him. After a stern look and a firm "No, I insist," he offered no argument. And people noticed.

Now, I wasn't too thrilled about stopping for one beer and eating a $100 check. (By the way, alcohol is not an expensable item for most retailers. I ate the bill.) Yet the lesson received by a great many people that night was worth every penny. Leaders need to model good behavior. It speaks volumes.

We'll Fill My Warehouse

Many vendors tend to work a relationship in small ways, and some get grander ideas. "Can you get me those orders this week instead of next? There's a sales contest on, and it would mean a lot to me." A little thing, but there is a cost in terms of inventory turn, payables, possible efficiency. Little costs add up to big costs. I once worked for an inventory director who was very chummy with the vendors. Drinks after work and tickets to football games were normal. One day, he instructed me to place four months' worth of orders (this vendor was a substantial paper manufacturer) as a "going away" gesture for William. It seems his good friend William was being promoted and, in the new position, would become a salaried employee rather than a commissioned employee. This last order would yield a substantial payday for someone who had been and would continue to be a good advocate for our company. Well, good for Willie, bad for everyone else. The company didn't need the inventory, and it cost us a lot of behind-the-scenes money. The buyer wanted to replace several SKUs a month later and was stunned that we had five months of inventory to mark down (another vendor unfairly had to pay for that markdown). Ironically, even the sales rep's own company suffered. The sales reps were paid solely on commission. William's replacement came in and realized that one of his largest accounts wouldn't be ordering for six months. And since William had asked the same favor of other inventory directors, the new sales rep found the same scenarios at his other large customers. He had to resign rather than go hungry for half the year.

I could easily fill another book with stories which cut to the heart of ethics and values. Every merchant will encounter similar choices.

When I terminated the young buyer for accepting a golf package to Las Vegas, I felt the infraction was so blatantly obvious that I had no qualms about my decision. I gained a key learning, however, when the young man pointed out that a vice president had gone to the Super Bowl and another executive had bragged about golfing on Augusta with a vendor. Is there a difference between their behavior and his? Why is it OK to have lunch with a vendor but not a trip to Vegas?

I've used the example of a student/teacher relationship to explain. A teacher can form a strong bond and get to know students on a personal level. You can have fun, be supportive, but a separation must remain. One is an adult. One is not. The arm's length needs to stay in place.

Ultimately, I think it comes down to experience within values. While I can provide instruction and direction, I often tell young up 'n' comers that I cannot give them experience. Until you've held the responsibility, dealt with the situation, corrected course based on circumstances, and so forth, you just cannot get it. Add to experience a values set that says, "I'm paid by company XYZ, and I am paid to always represent the best interests of the company." Perhaps more basic is simply the sense of right and wrong. Accepting money or favors will simply put the merchant in a position of compromise. And by the way, you will be fired. Is it worth losing the job?

So, why can the senior executive go to Augusta? Perhaps that person has the experience to deal with such a situation and not be compromised. At a senior level, the discussion is usually more strategic. Senior execs don't place orders or pick SKUs. Lastly, the senior exec, hopefully, got to be a senior exec because their value system is in line with the company's values. One caution: as long as younger employees look to their leaders as role models and learn from their behavior, the ambiguity needs explanation.

This subject is certainly less black and white than a Vendor Data Form. My hope is to provoke thought and a sense that morals and ethics play an important part in creating a great merchant. The subject also rises above the merchant. What's the value system within the company? Many larger retailers have a written ethics policy and review it with employees. Some attempt to remove the grey. Wal-Mart, for example, has a zero-tolerance approach. Employees can accept nothing from a vendor—no candy at Christmas, no dinners, not even a soda. This policy is very clear . . . no ambiguity. More tolerant companies recognize that something is missing in so stringent an approach. Others move their buyers to different categories every two years as a way to discourage getting too close to any vendor. So where does the line get drawn?

Passion and Reason

The passion side is the love of the game. This person has the Sunday newspaper delivered for the ads more than for the sports or news sections. On vacation, he still wanders in to the new retail concept because there's an insatiable desire to see the newest trend or a creative display. Still, this passion must be tempered with reason in order to be successful.

Several years ago, a young buyer on my team was showing great promise, and we orchestrated a lateral move for his development. About thirty days after the move, his replacement came to me to discuss the programs that had been negotiated by her predecessor. It seemed that our young "star" had neglected a few details.

The new buyer found a volume incentive that was contingent on our adding three new SKUs per quarter. Nice for the vendor, very limiting to us. She also found that many vendors had been pushed for better payment terms, but accounting had never been notified of the changes. Lastly, MDF forms were discovered that suggested support had been negotiated for numerous ads. The money went uncollected.

Moral of the story: *retail is detail!*

In my experience, I've seen this time and again. Talented, passionate dealmakers negotiate incredible programs, yet a lack of documentation and process makes it all for naught if allowances go uncollected. A great negotiator is not necessarily a great merchant.

The "reason" part of this equation is just as important as the passion. In preparing for a negotiation, the great merchant has done his homework. Facts are at hand, such as market share data, sales, gross margin, competitive shops, and industry projections for growth or decline. "If you're telling me this product will cost $6.50 each, why is Sam's Club selling it for $6.44?" The more sophisticated retailers build their assortments with their yearly sales plan in mind. The projections of sales and gross margin by SKU must yield the numbers needed to meet or beat the budget. This can actually dictate what a buyer is willing to pay for a product.

Blocking and Tackling

The great merchant is grounded in the basics. While this part is not glamorous, it's foundational to the trade. Just like a great architect needs paper, ruler, and pencil (maybe an eraser), the great painter needs canvas, paint, and brush, the merchant needs vendor data, and ad checkerboard, and allowance controls. While the game can be a lot of fun, it's first about making money. The inefficiency of not being detailed in the merchant chair can cost any company vast amounts of money. Here are some examples that I've seen:

1. Many companies don't keep basic vendor data (name, address, e-mail) in an orderly fashion. When the president needs to send out a communication he/she can either use the A/P address list (not a very good option) or ask the merchant team to provide the info. Usually pulling together such a list is a fire drill. Four months later, another announcement goes out, the list is requested again and again, the inefficiency is obvious.

2. Most new item setup forms will call for case-pack/inner-pack quantities, carton or unit weight, unit of measure,

and more. Inaccurate or missing data can inhibit shipping performance, sales, or even customer satisfaction.

I once experienced a company which had no discipline around item descriptions. Every buyer had their own style, their own abbreviations, and their own view of what they needed from a description. As the new guy, I pulled a SKU-level report on three-ring binders and saw . . .

- 3 Ring Binder
- 2 Pocket 3 Ring Binder—Blue
- 2 Pocket Binder—Rd
- Bndr, 3 Ring, BE
- WJ 3 Ring—GN
- Binder Green—Poly
- Binder—Vinyl 3 ring
- D Ring 2 Pocket BL

I could go on, but you probably get the point. Blue is represented as BE, BL, and Blue. Well, one day, the company decided to launch a website, and these descriptions became actual lines for the customer invoice. The entire item file had to be rewritten.

3.   Taking the Internet story further, another company used their item data to take the weight of each item and use it to calculate freight charges for their outbound orders. Unfortunately, the buyers had never really paid attention to this data field. It was meaningless to them, so rather than get accurate information, they usually just put in anything. The result was a six-figure loss on billing before the problem was identified and fixed.

What Makes a Merchant a Great Merchant?

I actually answered this question for myself in the spring of 1997 when two unrelated events took place. One was the loss of a job, and the second was (of all things) a sermon.

The job loss required that I prepare and organize a search for employment. In conducting my search and in going through multiple interviews, I discovered that the exceptional merchant (merchandise manager, category manager, buyer, etc.) had four key pieces in addition to the obvious basics like reading comprehension and math skills. A fifth characteristic was found in the sermon.

1. Organization—Organizational skills are a key ingredient for the great merchant. I'm sure the vendor community has had many a good laugh over succumbing to the pressure of a buyer to get a deeper deal only to find that the company never follows through to collect it. Or how many co-op dollars are left on the table because a buyer relies on memory rather than documentation? To be organized means that follow up, attention to detail, and documentation are tended to and practiced daily.

    Also, time is often the buyer's primary antagonist. Enormous amounts of work are done and then done again due to a lack of organization. The boss needs a vendor list, time to prepare a budget, and accounting needs a recap of all rebates. These daily intrusions are merely taken in stride for the organized professional yet become obstacles and time consumers for the disorganized.

2. Communication—The great merchant is a good communicator and has sound written and verbal skills. As the focal point for every retail or mail-order organization, the buyer or merchant must not only procure goods but communicate with stores, operations management, accounting, loss prevention, senior management, and of course, the vendor, just to name a few. No Surprises are words to live by.

3. Study—The great merchant does his homework. He shops competition. He studies the industry, the trends, the publications related to his business. Keeping a supplier honest requires looking at their competition.

    Retail has evolved and become substantially more complicated over the past twenty-five years. Manufacturers often need to market to multiple channels (mass, drug, grocery, clubs), and each channel has major players that want to believe that "their" deal is better than anyone else's. In fact, if I'm Wal-Mart in the mass or Office

Max in office products or Home Depot in the building-products channel, I virtually demand a better price than the other guys. Somehow, manufacturers must put together programs to address this as fairly as possible, and the merchant will only have a good sense of where he stands if he does his homework.

4.   Guts—A great merchant needs the guts to make a decision. Many manufacturers have told me that more than anything else, they like a buyer that can make a decision. "Tell me no as long as you tell me something."

In many companies, the merchandise manager may have responsibility for as much as 25 to 35% of a company's business. That's significant for even a modest retailer. In a Best Buy, Comp USA, Home Depot, Office Depot, K-Mart, or Sam's Club, the numbers become staggering. Buying a widget may require a six- or even seven-figure purchase. If you don't buy enough, you're a bum, and the heat comes down for not maximizing sales or meeting the needs of an ad. If you buy too much, you're a bum, and stores don't have the room for residuals. Associates will want to see markdowns. People will want to know how you will get out of the excess inventory. Yes, it takes guts to buy fresh product.

The final element of being a great merchant was served up to me by the Pastor of St. Charles Church in Boardman, Ohio. In the liturgical calendar, Good Shepherd's Sunday follows shortly after Easter. I'm sure most people have heard a "Good Shepherd" story or two, and on this occasion, Father Dan had his version. He told us about a party he had attended at which two people were asked to read the Psalm of the Good Shepherd. The first man was a trained Shakespearean actor. His locution, perfect enunciation, and deep voice were mesmerizing. He read the piece aloud and brought all his skills to bare. The crowd responded with riotous applause.

The second speaker, a minister, was certainly intimidated. This would be a tough act to follow. Still, he addressed the group and read the Psalm. When he finished, the people were weeping rather than applauding. Although his skills were not on the level of the Shakespearean actor, to the minister, this was more than the reading of a part. This was his life, his mission. The actor turned to the gathering and said, "My skills, no matter how extraordinary, can only tell you about the Good Shepherd. This man is the Good Shepherd."

The bottom line here is PASSION. The truly great merchant has a passion for his calling much like the shepherd. Buying becomes more than a job, it becomes your profession. It's the passion that has you reading the Sunday ads even on your vacation. It's the rush a true merchant gets from a successful strategy, an ad that blows away projection, or a deal that sets you apart in the marketplace.

Although they are becoming more of a rare breed, behind the really successful retailers, you will find some truly great merchants.

INDEX